FEB - - 2003

W I

ROCK
MY
SOUL

Also by bell hooks

ROCK
MY
SOUL

BLACK PEOPLE AND SELF-ESTEEM

bell hooks

ATRIA BOOKS

New York London Toronto Sydney Singapore

ATRIA BOOKS
1230 Avenue of the Americas
New York, NY 10020

ISBN: 0-7434-5605-X

First Atria Books hardcover printing January 2003

10   9   8   7   6   5   4   3   2   1

ATRIA BOOKS is a trademark of Simon & Schuster, Inc.

For information regarding special discounts for bulk purchases,
please contact Simon & Schuster Special Sales at 1-800-456-6798
or business@simonandschuster.com

Printed in the U.S.A.

What do you mean, project a good image? An image to who? Who don't like the image I project? That's the weakest thing I've heard yet; I'm not a good image. For my people, I'm the best image in the world.

—Muhammad Ali

Contents

Touch me on the inside part and call me my name . . .
—Toni Morrison, *Beloved*

PREFACE

The Inside Part:
Self-Esteem Today

A few years ago, a national news magazine had a cover story with the heading, WHATEVER HAPPENED TO BLACK AMERICA? I leafed through the pages at a newsstand, scanning the statistics about joblessness, welfare mothers, divorce rates, drug addiction, and put it down, recognizing that the stories the writers chose to tell about black American life were the ones that would support and affirm the notion that very little of interest to anyone was happening in black life. As a cultural critic writing about the representation of blackness in mass media, I was stunned—enraged—by this construction of blackness. I felt powerless in the face of the powerful white folks running this magazine who could decide to announce the disappearance, the death of an entire race to sell magazines.

Self-congratulatory in tone, the stories' gist was that black folks had wiped themselves out, had committed a collective cultural genocide, that "we gave them rights and opportunity and look what they did with it." Such sentiments were common in the wake of affirmative-action backlash. Once you publicly pronounce that a people are culturally gone, no longer there to be looked at, gazed upon, or talked about, then you rid yourself of the issue of accountability. You announce their doom and tell the world that they chose this fate—passive disappearance, silent self-sabotage, symbolic suicide. Daringly you expose their secret shame. And the source of that shame was that with so much going for them black folks had done so little. And racism was not to blame.

If racism was not to blame for a lack of progress in black life, then what could the issue be? No one seemed then or in recent times to be able to answer that question. While I never accepted the notion that black people had disappeared, I had begun to wonder why we were not doing more and why with so much opportunity and success on all fronts there was so much suffering in the lives of black folks. The suffering was not limited to the poor and the underclass. It had and has no relation to how much money we are making or how successful we are.

Long before I began to look around me and saw how widespread this underlying emotional distress was, I saw it first in the students I encountered at the Ivy League institutions where I taught. They were among the best and the brightest and oftentimes the beautiful, yet they were beset by deep feelings of unworthiness, of ugliness inside and outside. They were overwhelmed by all the choices before them and unable to assert meaningful agency. More often than not they were depressed without knowing why, drugs—whether illegal or prescription—did not solve the problem, and there were more attempted suicides than anyone cared to talk about.

From the very first moment I listened to their stories, whether in my office, on my couch at home, or in hospital rooms, what I heard voiced was a profound lack of self-esteem. And when I listened to my peers, the generation of baby boomers who had excelled and made their mark, I heard similar narratives. I heard folks talk about deep feelings of inadequacy, of not being "enough," even when they could not define what the enough would be. I heard and hear feelings of shame, guilt, inferiority. Finally, after hearing confessions of self-loathing and self-distrust, I was compelled to face the reality underlying this testimony. I wanted to do something, to find the explanations and the solutions. From all my research I returned again and again to the issue of self-esteem.

African Americans have collectively grappled with the issue of self-esteem from slavery to the present day. One of the growing causes of alarm has been the intensification of low self-esteem in the face of all manner of opportunities that were not there for our ancestors. And though racism and white supremacy are still the order of the day, they are not as powerful determinants of our lot in life as they once were. Looking at my family, I have often pondered why my brother, my five sisters, and I seemed to be way more psychologically fragile than our parents before us. Like in many southern black families where education had been pushed, we had all studied, learned, earned degrees, made money. And while all our lives we have had a level of material privilege that our parents had not known, material gain had not served to change basic self-concepts. Again and again in our conversations we returned to the issue of self-esteem.

None of us imagine that we can go to a doctor who will give us a prescription for healing without first examining us to find the roots of our problem. In *Rock My Soul: Black People and Self-Esteem* this is the path I take: rigorous examination of the issue concluding with suggestions of what we can do. Throughout *Rock My Soul* I rely on the work of psychologist Nathaniel Branden to provide useful definitions of self-esteem that have stood the test of time. He explains: "Self-esteem, fully realized, is the experience that we are appropriate to life and to the requirements of life. . . . Self-esteem is confidence in our ability to think; confidence in our ability to cope with the basic challenges of life; and confidence in our right to be successful and happy; the feeling of being worthy, deserving, entitled to assert our needs and wants, achieve our values, and enjoy the fruits of our efforts." Branden identified six pillars of self-esteem: personal integrity, self-acceptance, self-responsibility, self-assertion, living consciously, and living purposefully. Without self-esteem people begin to lose their sense of agency. They feel powerless. They feel they can only be victims. The need for self-esteem never goes away. And it is never too late for us to acquire the healthy self-esteem that is needed if we are to have fulfilling lives.

We black folks have been unwilling to break through our denial and deal with the truth that crippling low self-esteem has reached epidemic proportions in our lives because it seems like it's just not a deep enough diagnosis. Again and again in books and articles written by black thinkers, the authors detail a long list of ailments that imply a crisis of self-esteem, then refuse to see our suffering as connected primarily to a lack of self-esteem, because as one writer puts it, this is just "too simplistic." The diagnosis may be a simple one, but clearly it has not been a simple task for us to build sustained foundations for the construction of healthy self-esteem in black life, because if that were the case there would be no crisis. Often we have focused so much on how others wound our self-esteem that we have overlooked the wounds that are self-inflicted. To attend to those wounds, to learn how to embrace emotional well-being without self-sabotaging, we need to pay closer attention to the issue of self-respect. We need to highlight the issue of self-esteem.

Although we may have had a long period of silence, maybe

even denial, when we have been unable to speak openly and honestly about the crisis in how we see ourselves and others and how we are seen, we black folks know that our collective wounded self-esteem has not been healed. We know that we are in pain. And it is only through facing the pain that we will be able to make it go away.

1

Healing Wounded Hearts

Self-esteem is not a sexy term. For many folks it conjures up images of self-help issues that were popular "back in the day." Indeed, in our nation public talk about self-esteem was at its highest in the sixties. Then the United States, one of the most powerful and wealthy nations in the world, was producing citizens who were simply discontent with their lot in life, who saw themselves as failures. Many of these individuals had come from upper-class backgrounds, were educated at the best schools, prospered in jobs and careers, moved in elite social circles, and yet found themselves unable to feel truly successful or enjoy life. They went to psychologists seeking a way to gain health for the mind. These individuals were white Americans. Psychology of the fifties had little to say about the psyches and souls of black folks.

In 1954 Nathaniel Branden had a small psychotherapy practice. His clients were all white but from diverse class backgrounds. Working with their issues, he began to focus on the issue of self-esteem. Branden recalls: "Reflecting on the stories I heard from clients, I looked for a common denominator, and I was struck by the fact that whatever the person's particular complaint, there was always a deeper issue: a sense of inadequacy, of not being 'enough,' a feeling of guilt or shame or inferiority, a clear lack of self-acceptance, self-trust, and self-love. In other words, a problem of self-esteem." He published his first articles on the psychology of self-esteem in the sixties.

Racial integration was hotly debated in the early sixties. The issue of whether black people were inferior to whites and therefore would be unable to do well in an integrated work or school context was commonly discussed. Racist white folks insisted everyone did better when they stayed with their own kind. And there were black folks who agreed with them. When the issue of self-esteem was raised in relation to black people, it was just assumed that racism was the primary factor creating low self-esteem. Consequently, when black public figures, most of whom were male at the time, began to address the issue of self-esteem, they focused solely on the impact of racism as a force that crippled our self-esteem.

Militant antiracist political struggles placed the issue of self-esteem for black folks on the agenda. And it took the form of primarily discussing the need for positive images. The slogan "black is beautiful" was popularized in an effort to undo the negative racist iconography and representations of blackness that had been an accepted norm in visual culture. Natural hairstyles were offered to counter the negative stereotype that one could be beautiful only if one's hair was straight and not kinky. "Happy to be nappy" was also a popular slogan among militant black liberation groups. Even black folks whose hair was not naturally kinky found ways to make their hair look nappy to be part of the black-is-beautiful movement. Capitalist entrepeneurs, white and black, welcomed the creation of a new market—that is, material goods related to black pride (African clothing, picks for hair, black dolls). Market forces were pleased to support the aspect of black pride that was all about new commodities.

Now pride in blackness already existed in every black community in the United States. While its cultural power may never have eliminated internalized racial self-hatred, the movement for racial uplift that began the moment individual free black folks came to the "New World," combined with the force of slave resistance, had already established the cultural foundations for black pride way before the fifties, even though the term *self-esteem* was not a part of the popular discourse of racial uplift. Writing on the subject of black pride in "Credo" in 1904, W. E. B. Du Bois declared,

> I believe in pride of race and lineage and self.... I believe in Liberty for all men, the space to stretch their arms and their souls, the right to breathe and the right to vote, the freedom to choose their friends, enjoy the sunshine, and the right to vote, the freedom to choose their friends, enjoy the sunshine and ride on the railroads, uncursed by color; thinking, dreaming, working as they will in a kingdom of God and Love. I believe in the training of children, black even as white; the leading out of little souls into the green pastures and beside the still waters, not for self, or peace, but for Life lit by some large vision of beauty and goodness and truth.

Du Bois advocated working for racial uplift because he was not afraid to examine the ways racism had kept black folks from fully realizing their potential for human development.

This same demand for holistic self-development rooted in black pride was the foundation of the black women's club movement. Speaking in 1916 on the subject of "The Modern Woman," black woman leader Mary Church Terrell shared her vision of the special mission of educated black women: "We have to do more than other women. Those of us fortunate enough to have education must share it with the less fortunate of our race. We must go into our communities and improve them; we must go out into the nation and change it. Above all, we must organize ourselves as Negro women and work together." A militant spirit of racial uplift was the unifying principle of the black women's club movement throughout the nation. The issue was not just to confront and resist racism but to create a culture of freedom and possiblity that would enable all black folks irrespective of class to engage in constructive self-help.

The call for racial uplift in the early twentieth century was not a superficial evocation of black pride; instead it was truly a call for this newly freed mass population of Americans, African and those of African descent, to strive to be fully self-actualized. To some extent the black pride movement of the sixties, with its intense focus on representation, shifted attention away from the moral and ethical demands of racial uplift, its spiritual dimension, and focused solely on the issue of gaining equality with whites. The psyches and souls of black folks needed to be nourished as much as did the individual's need for material goods and basic civil rights in the public sphere. Yet more often than not the inner psychological development of black folks was ignored by those black public figures who were most concerned with gaining equal access within the existing social system.

No wonder then that after major civil rights were gained and militant black power movement had increased social and economic opportunities, the focus on black pride diminished. The need for an organized ongoing program of racial uplift, though acknowledged, never gained meaningful momentum. This may have been a direct consequence of the waning power of black female leadership, especially the political leadership fostered by the black women's club movement. Though often guilty of class elitism, black women in the club movement held values focused on holistic self-development for black people of all classes. Black folks were encouraged to have proper etiquette and manners, to be people of integrity, to educate themselves, to work hard, to be religious, and to value service to others. Indeed, the phrase "racial uplift through self-help" was a common slogan used in black women's organizations.

In the early twentieth century prominent black male leaders began to demand of black women that they cease working in an egalitarian manner alongside black men for racial uplift. This demand changed the tenor and tone of black civil rights struggle. In the twenties patriarchal black male leaders pointedly told black women to step back from the social and political realms. Black nationalism became the vehicle to push black patriarchal values. As a new leader Marcus Garvey used his newspaper, *The Negro World,* to advocate sexist thinking about the nature of women's role. Articles ran in the paper urging black folks to "go back to the days of true manhood when women truly reverenced us." This resistance to partnership in struggle reached a peak in the early sixties.

When Daniel Patrick Moynihan, in his role as assistant secretary of labor, wrote the report "The Negro Family: The Case for National Action," his intent, as explained in *Too Heavy a Load* by historian Deborah Gray White, was "to alert government policy makers to the problems in black America that went beyond desegreation and voting." She contends: "He aimed to demonstrate that neither the Civil Rights movement nor Civil Rights legislation had made an impact on black everyday life. Indeed, the report's survey of unemployment, housing, school dropout rates, crime and delinquency, and intelligence tests revealed that over ten years of Civil Rights protests and national upheaval had not changed the fundamental living conditions of most African-Americans."

Following in the wake of conservative black male patriarchs (in particular the sociologist John Hope Franklin), Moynihan felt the key to black underdevelopment was the lack of patriarchal gender arrangements in black homes. In his report he stated: "Ours is a society which presumes male leadership in private and public affairs. The arrangements of society facilitate and reward it. A subculture, such as that of the Negro American, in which this is not the pattern, is placed at a distinct disadvantage." When black liberation struggle moved from a focus on mutual racial uplift of black males and females to an insistence that black men dominate and black women maintain a subordinate position, the focus on holistic development shifted to gaining equality with white men. Civil rights movement coupled with militant, patriarchal black liberation struggle successfully challenged the nation so that black people gained greater rights. Racial integration effectively created a cultural context where it was at least clearer to everyone that given equal opportunity, black citizens would excel or fail depending on circumstance just like white citizens.

Ulitmately, like their white counterparts, black folks in this nation gained greater economic privileges, civil rights, all manner of equality, and yet found that even with all these progressive changes all was not well with their souls, that many of them were lacking in self-esteem. In many cases black females subordinated themselves to black males, but black men were still discontent. Two-parent black families had many of the same woes as single-parent homes. Yet while white folks were looking to progressive psychology to soothe their psyches, their discontent, black leaders more than ever before in African-American history named racism as the central culprit disturbing the peace in our lives.

These same leaders responded to struggles for gender equality by acting as though greater freedom for black females was a covert attack on black males. Prior to such thinking it was merely assumed that any gains black females made were gains for the race as a whole. In all their activism black women in the early part of the twentieth century continually insisted that gender equality enhanced the struggle for black liberation. Such thinking lost momentum as patriarchal thinking became more an accepted norm for black males and females. Militant black power Panther spokesperson Eldridge Cleaver told the world in his 1968 international bestseller *Soul on Ice* that the black woman was the "silent ally . . . of the white man," who used her to destroy black manhood. Labeling black females "race traitors" should have galvanized masses of black females and males to protest. Instead, there was widespread agreement on the part of black males and females who were socialized to accept patriarchal thinking without question that black male development would be furthered by the subordination of black women.

Plenty of political black women responded to the black male insistence that patriarchal domination by black men was the only way to heal the wounds of racism by standing behind their men. Activist Margaret Wright clearly saw the contradictions: "Black men used to admire the black woman for all they'd endured to keep the race going. Now the black man is saying he wants a family structure like the white man's. He's got to be head of the family and women have to be submissive and all that nonsense . . . the white woman is already oppressed in that setup." The lone individuals, female and male, who had the foresight to see that gender warfare would undermine the historical solidarity in struggle between black women and men and lead to more havoc in black family life could not sway political opinion in a progressive direction.

Black women who joined feminist movement, whether in separatist or integrated contexts, risked being labeled race traitors, but that did not lead to silence. By the late seventies and early eighties individual black women active in feminist movement were making our voices heard loud and clear, but we were no longer recognized as leaders or would-be leaders in our diverse black communities. Just supporting feminism, and using the word, allowed many black folks to ignore the valid social and political critiques that we were making.

Being labeled a race traitor was devastating to the self-esteem of black women who had found in antiracist struggle a basis on which to build positive self-concepts. To be told that the black woman's efforts to end racism were detrimental to the race was incredibly confusing to many black females. Black nationalism alone did not give credence to patriarchal thinking. Fundamentalist Christian thinking about gender roles had been deeply embedded in the social thought of black folks from slavery on into freedom. That rhetoric joined with the patriarchal rhetoric of conservative black nationalism, reinforcing in the minds and hearts of black males and females alike that male domination of women should be the norm.

Ironically, the insistence that patriarchy would heal the wounds inflicted by white supremacy and racial terrorism gained momentum at precisely that historical moment when affluent white women were telling the world that all was not well in the homes of Dick and Jane. Domestic violence, incest, depression, and all manner of addiction and mental illness were identified as the plight white females suffered in affluent marriages. Concurrently, feminist movement made it possible for more men than ever before in our nation to protest the way patriarchal masculinity crippled the psyches and souls of men. Progressive white men questioning patriarchy were not listened to by black males who wanted patriarchal power. The equation of power with self-esteem was the faulty thinking that would ultimately trap black males.

Even though Martin Luther King, Jr., had warned black folks and all citizens of this nation in his collection of sermons *Strength to Love,* first published in 1963, that we would endanger our souls if we ignored the interrelatedness of all life, if we chose violence over peace, hatred over love, materialism over communalism, his words were not fully embraced. Yet his insights were clearly prophetic. Now, more than thirty years later, his declaration that "we have foolishly minimized the internal of our lives and maximized the external" accurately defines the collective condition of African-American life today. King admonished:

> We will not find peace in our generation until we learn anew that a man's life consisteth not in the abundance of things which he possesseth, but in those inner treasures for the spirit. . . . Our hope for creative living lies in our ability to establish the spiritual ends of our lives in personal character and social justice. Without this spiritual and moral reawakening we shall destroy ourselves in the misuse of our own instruments. Our generation cannot escape the question of our Lord: What shall it profit a man, if he gain the whole world of exter-

nals—aeroplanes, electric lights, automoblies, and color television—and lose the internal—his own soul?

The brutal assassinations of Martin Luther King, Jr., and Malcolm X silenced public political discourse about the souls of black folks. Psychologists wrote no books about the collective depression and despair generated by the hopelessness of these deaths or the collective grief earned by the loss of the belief that love would conquer hate, that democracy and freedom would rule the day. While the world witnessed the collective public grief of this nation when liberal and progressive leaders were slaughtered one after the other, no one attended to the private despair of African Americans who felt the dream of beloved community, of ending racism, was never to be realized.

Many young white people shared this grief, this sense of profound disillusionment with our nation. The war in Vietnam shattered the assumption that our government supported freedom. The tyranny of imperialist white supremacist patriarchal violence around the world and here at home crushed spirits. In the aftermath of this disillusionment black and white folk alike became obsessed with material security. When the seventies ended, it was popularly accepted that material goods and the acquisition of power within the existing structure of our society was more attainable than freedom. And if one could not attain power and privilege, one eased the pain with addictions: drugs, alcohol, food, sex, shopping.

Capitalism and market forces welcomed black folk into the world of hedonistic consumerism. Rather than worry our minds and hearts about social justice, antiracist struggle, women's liberation, the plight of the poor, or the failure of democratic principles, black people were urged to see consumption as the way to define success and well-being. The very "externals" King had warned about had come to be seen as the measure of the content of our character and the quality of our lives. Patriarchal black public figures, male and female, placed all their emphasis on material goals. In the contemporary black church folks bowed down to the god of prosperity and lost interest in the god of service. Black communities began to let go the distinct ethical, moral, and spiritual beliefs that for so long had formed the foundation of black life. Yet still our leaders talked mainly about the impact of racism. The patriarchal men and women who had not supported black liberation struggle rooted in feminist thinking rarely spoke about the reality that the emergence of patriarchal black families had not led to greater well-being in African-American life.

A child of the fifties in that part of the American south that was always seen as culturally backward, I was raised in a world where racial uplift was the norm. Like their nineteenth-century ancestors, our working-class parents believed that if we wanted freedom we had to be worthy of it, that we had to educate ourselves, work hard, be people of integrity. Racial uplift through self-help meant not just that we should confront racism, we should become fully cultured holistic individuals. Even though my family did not have much money, we were encouraged to work odd jobs so that we could pay for lessons and learn to play musical instruments. Reading was encouraged. Education was the way to freedom. Educated, we would not necessarily change how the white world saw us, but we would change how we saw ourselves. Even so, my parents and the other black folks in our community never behaved as though education alone was the key to a successful life. We had to nourish our souls through spiritual life, through service to others. We would create glory in our lives and let our light shine brightly for the world to see.

These were the values taught to me and my siblings by our parents and reinforced by the segregated schools and churches we attended. They were the values that had led to the creation, from slavery on, of a distinct African-American culture, a culture rooted in soulfulness, a culture of resistance where regardless of status, of whether one was bound or free, rich or poor, it was possible to triumph over dehumanization. This soulful black culture of resistance was rooted in hope. It had at its heart a love ethic. In this subculture of soul, individual black folks found ways to decolonize their minds and build healthy self-esteem. This showed us that we did not have to change externals to be self-loving. This soulful culture was most dynamically expressed during racial segregation because away from white supremacist control black folks could invent themselves.

Bringing an end to segregation had been a central part of civil rights struggle. And it was only when that struggle was won that our people began to collectively wonder if racial integration would really be the means to end racism, or would it be the beginning of a collective soul murder that would result in black people losing their hold on life. Our parents' debate over whether the closing of all-black schools would be progress or would give greater control of our lives over to white folks was one of the few intense political discussions I heard in my family. And it was from these discussions that Rosa Bell, our mama, would say, "You can want what white folk have to offer, but you don't have to love them." Having lived in the midst of white supremacy all her life, Mama recognized that it would be dangerous for us to live our lives trying to please racist white people, letting them set the standards for our identity and well-being.

Her words of caution proved to be necessary wisdom. While she wanted her children to have equal access to libraries and typewriters, small classrooms, and the newest textbooks, she did not want us to be taught by unenlightened white people to hate ourselves. She did not want her academically gifted children to let white people teach them they were the grand exceptions, better than other black folks, maybe even not really black. The self-esteem that had been fostered in a social and political atmosphere of racial uplift was assaulted in the world of racial integration. Black folks living in segregated worlds who had spent only a measure of their lives thinking about white folks were more and more becoming obssessed with race. Naturally, the more contact we had with white folks the more intensely we experienced racist assaults. Even the well-meaning and kind white teachers often believed racist stereotypes. We were never away from the surveillance of white supremacy in the world of racial integration. And it was this constant reality that began to undermine the foundation of self-esteem in the lives of black folks.

Throughout my undergraduate and graduate years, I spent my time in predominantly white colleges resisting racism in all its forms while carving subculture space for me to read my Emily Dickinson without some white person questioning my love of her work. In the all-black world of my growing up, I was never made to feel that my love of Shakespeare, of the Romantic poets, of Emily Dickinson, was weird. Learning was natural and loving great writing was natural. It was not a black or white thing to do, it was the thing to do because it was the way to improve one's lot in life economically and culturally.

It was in the context of whiteness that I was encouraged to

see myself as separate from other black people, better somehow because I was intelligent. Now this thinking ran counter to everything my parents had taught me. And I resisted it, as did the few black peers I would have as classmates. We were always turning to our roots for affirmation and sustenance, to traditional black folks culture. That subculture was not powerful simply because our skin was dark; it was powerful because it was a culture of resistance, a world where our self-esteem and our soulfulness was nurtured.

The false, segregated culture created by contemporary black nationalism was rarely a culture of ongoing progressive resistance. Informed by the tenets of patriarchal violence, it was not a safe place for black females or homosexual black males. The segregated black culture of American apartheid was never chosen by black folks or held up as the best way to live. In his writings W. E. B. Du Bois urged black folks to see ourselves as citizens of the world, valuing our race but remaining open to a world beyond our race. Within traditional segregated southern black folk culture we found refuge from the intensity of white racism. Racial integration brought us face-to-face with the possibility of racist assault or an actual confrontation.

No psychologists rushed to study the impact on the black psyche of moving from racial segregation to an integrated world. Since the logic of white supremacist thinking had made it seem that black people were longing to be close to white folks, it was not possible for our fears to gain a hearing. In the most recent global history of race and racism, the end of racial apartheid in South Africa did generate discussion about the way black people experienced newfound freedoms. Yet there is no abundant testimony in American history that documents the way black people felt internally about suddenly being in close contact with white people on a basis other than domination. In my own work I have documented the fear of whiteness that was instilled in me as a child, a fear generated by the knowledge that white people could terrorize black folks with impunity. We did not just imagine that this could happen; this was black experience in the heart of southern racial apartheid. My sisters and brother and I were in our teens when schools were desegregated. We were afraid for our lives in ways that were no doubt exaggerated, but our fear was real. And it created stress. I felt that the major difference in attending a segregated school, rather than a predominantly white school where the administrative power was all white and male, was the level of stress I felt. The fear lurking in the corridors. The fear of racial unrest and upheaval. If black children could not see the predominantly white classroom as a safe place, then how we could relax enough to learn there—to excel?

I survived and did well in those classrooms not because racism was not present but because I knew that ultimately a bell would ring and I would be free to enter a world of warmth and care that was all black and welcoming. I could be reunited with my brother, whom I rarely saw in our white schools. Black males who had been gifted students in our black schools were usually not selected to be in the gifted classes in the white schools because their presence might be a threat to white womanhood. All the smart black boys that surrounded me in grade school and in junior high vanished with the integration of high schools. Their "disappearance" was political. And it generated fear in me. Often I would lay my head on the desk in history class and weep. I wept for the world that had been taken from us, schools where our teachers loved us, where we were together, where no one doubted our capacity to learn or called into question our interest in learning.

Too late we learned that while much might have been substandard in those segregated schools (that is, buildings, textbooks, equipment, etc.), what was first-rate was the expectation that we would all be learners, that there existed geniuses and slow learners among us, but no one thought that to educate oneself to the fullest would alienate you from blackness. In predominantly white schools, set apart from African-American peers but never accepted fully by white students, smart black kids often began a journey into the abyss of self-doubt. Now self-doubt has practically become the norm among black children of all classes. Segregation is clearly not the answer. Yet it is easier to segregate children than to make the fundamental changes in our educational system that would make it possible for everyone to have faith in their capacity to learn, to excel.

When I was a college student most of the black students I knew were striving hard to excel. At times crippling self-doubt, often engendered by the way we were treated by unenlightened professors, white and nonwhite, chipped away at self-esteem, and students who had once worked hard to overachieve began to falter and fail. More often than not failures were seen as solely a consequence of racism. It was easier to highlight racism than to examine holistically the construction of our self-concepts and self-esteem. It was not that racism was not an issue, it was the reality that it was not the only issue that was often obscured. Certainly, many of us had been given the skills in our all-black subcultures to stand strong in the midst of racial assault, but rarely did anyone speak to the issue of low self-esteem among the best and the brightest, of the psychological problems that beset us that had nothing directly to do with race or racism.

The assumption that African-American overachievers have

positive self-esteem is so deeply implanted in the minds of most people that it is difficult for us to identify the problems successful folks may face with self-concept or self-regard. And of course when anyone looks at black folks who are not materially privileged it is just assumed that poverty leads to crippling self-esteem. While there have been a spate of books recently that seek to explain "self-sabotage in black America," insisting that the problem is not racism, there is still little discussion of the role self-esteem plays in self-development and overall well-being.

Teaching at Oberlin, Yale, and at public institutions like City College, I encountered a broad spectrum of brilliant young black students from varying class backgrounds and social circumstances. Yet they seemed to have in common low self-regard. Whether they came from materially privileged homes, where they had access to everything money could buy and seemingly doting parents, homes where Mom and Dad were both present, or from working-class and poor single-parent homes, they seemed to share a grave sense of self-doubt. Many of them saw the problem of crippling low self-esteem in their lives as stemming from the expectations that they should be high achievers, that they should excel always. It was easier for these students to call attention to the ways racism had been a factor in their self-doubt than it was for them to look at other issues in family life that might have affected their self-concept and self-esteem.

A few years ago I bgan to think about the place of love in African-American life, to look critically at the way success for black people has been increasingly measured by a limited yardstick, one that primarily looks at material wealth and acquisition as the sole sign of well-being. As King had prophesied, black folks of all classes seemed to be most concerned with money and the things that money could buy. Discussing racism was often deemed important only to the extent that racism was perceived as blocking access to material well-being. Care of the soul was simply not a priority on the agendas set by public figures and political leaders who claimed, and claim, to be concerned about saving the race.

The one place where individual black folk were raising questions about our being was in feminist-based black women's organizations and organizations that focused on issues of black women's health. As was the case in the early part of the twentieth century, individual black women more than black men were calling for a holistic evaluation of our self-concepts, one that would place psychological well-being above status and making money. In 1993 I published *Sisters of the Yam: Black Women and Self-Recovery,* including in it a chapter called "Living to Love" wherein I attempted to link issues of self-esteem with progressive antiracist, anticlassist political resistance. I argued:

> Given the politics of black life in this white supremacist society it makes sense that internalized racism and self-hate stand in the way of love. Systems of domination exploit folks best when they deprive us of our capacity to experience our own agency and alter our ability to care and to love ourselves and others. Black folks have been deeply and profoundly "hurt," as we used to say down home, "hurt to our hearts," and the deep psychological pain we have endured and still endure affects our capacity to feel and therefore our capacity to love. We are a wounded people. Wounded in that part of ourselves that would know love, that would be lov-

ing. The choice to love has always been a gesture of resistance for African Americans.

This work was the catalyst for me to begin a more intense exploration of lovelessness in American life, which culminated in the work *All about Love: New Visions*. In this work I talked about the growing cynicism in our nation about love and the way in which materialist greed and the yearning for wealth have become the order of that day. My next work, *Salvation: Black People and Love*, was a closer examination of the particular way in which the absence of a love ethic impacts on the social welfare and emotional well-being of African Americans. In the chapter "Moving Beyond Shame" I state: "The practice of self-love is difficult for everyone in a society that is more concerned with profit than well-being, but it is even more dificult for black folks, as we must constantly resist the negative perceptions of blackness we are encouraged to embrace by the dominant culture." Again and again when I spoke with individual black folks about why they were finding it difficult to practice self-love, we would find ourselves focusing on the issue of self-esteem.

Without a core foundation of healthy self-esteem we cannot practice self-love. In *Salvation* I did not emphasize enough the importance of creating healthy self-esteem. Folks with positive self-esteem know that there are a number of factors that shape and inform our emotional well-being. We know that while race and racism may overdetermine many aspects of our lives, we are still free to be self-determining. Many young black folks who are full of self-doubt and lacking in self-esteem fixate on race in a way that is demoralizing and dehumanizing. To a grave extent they project all their problems onto the landscape of racism because it is the easy target.

Though race is a vital aspect of our identity as African Americans, we cannot know ourselves fully if we look only at race. Looking at ourselves holistically, seeing our emotional well-being as rooted both in the politics of race and racism as well as in our capacity to be self-defining, we can create the self-esteem that is needed for us to care for our souls. In the black church of my youth we would sing the lyrics "is it well with your soul, are you free and made whole." Our continued survival as African-American people, in solidarity with non-black allies in struggle, demands that we care for our souls so that we can be whole and complete. If we begin with self-esteem our success is assured. Well-being will be our destiny.

2

Lasting Trauma

Most discussions of black people and self-esteem start by identifying racism as the sole culprit. Certainly the politics of race and racism impinge on our capacity as black folk to create self-love rooted in healthy self-esteem, sometimes in an absolute and brutal manner. Yet many of us create healthy self-esteem in a world where white supremacy and racism remain the norm. Clearly, being victims of racism does not imply that we cannot resist in ways that are an expression of healthy self-esteem. When we study the psychohistory of African Americans it becomes apparent that the foundation of the shaky self-esteem that assaults our sensibilities is rooted in the experience of traumatic violence. Whether it is the emotional violence caused by the pain of abandonment or the violence that is a consequence of domination (whether racism, sexism, or class elitism), it is the normalization of violence in our lives as black people that creates the foundation for ongoing trauma reenactment.

This violence and its impact on our collective and individual psychology has a long and silent history, one marked by the trauma of abuse and abandonment. At various historical moments scholars and social critics have called attention to the psychological consequences of trauma in relation to African-American emotional well-being, especially when talk-but the impact of racism, but we have yet to produce a substantial body of work in our society that truly honors the psychological traumas black people have collectively and individually experienced as a result of oppressive violence (especially as a consequence of racism and white supremacism both distinct from and combined with other forces of domination, for example, sexism).

By ignoring the fact that the context for psychological well-being has, more often than not, been absent in many of our lives, the notion that black folks heroically and magically triumphed over generations of genocidal assaults and everyday racism continues to prevail despite all the evidence that suggests otherwise. While books like psychologist Frantz Fanon's *Black Skin, White Masks* and the psychiatrists William Grier and Price Cobbs's *Black Rage,* which were published in the late sixties, offered analysis of black experience using a psychoanalytic perspective, they did not encourage masses of black folks to consider mental health care a fundamental part of liberation struggle. Fanon unabashedly declared in the introduction to *Black Skin, White Masks* his belief that "only a psychoanalytical interpretation of the black problem would shed light on the complexity of racialized subordination." Yet he was quick to add: "The analysis that I am undertaking is psychological. In spite of this it is apparent to me that the effective disalienation of the black man entails an immediate recognition of social and economic realities." And on the back cover reviewer Robert Coles declares that "no psychological 'defense' will enable the Negro to feel 'secure' or 'himself' until he is no longer the white man's social and economic prey." As political leadership around the issue of race has become patriarchal both in representation and message from the late sixties to the present day, there has been no meaningful recognition of the prolonged impact of psychological trauma on black experience. Yet this impact must be continually analyzed as well as the understanding of how folks recover from trauma shared.

Science and pseudoscience were used as part of the arguments for both the colonization of black people via slavery and the continued subordination of black folks from manumission on to the present day. Consequently, it is not surprising that masses of black people view science of the mind as suspect. Psychology has been especially feared because many black folks worry that speaking of our traumas using the language of mental illness will lead to biased interpretation and to the pathologizing of black experience in ways that might support and sustain our continued subordination. To a grave extent African Americans have colluded with the dominant culture in refusing to document in a substantive way the ongoing psychological impact of traumatic violence. Throughout our history in this nation, black people and society as a whole have wanted to minimize the reality of trauma in black life. It has been easier for everyone to focus on issues of material survival and see material deprivation as the reason for our continued collective subordinated status than to place the issue of trauma and recovery on our agendas.

While individual scholars and practitioners in the mental health field have produced outstanding work aimed at addressing the psychological ills that particularly beset black folks, there just is not enough work being done, and very little done from a progressive standpoint, one that starts with a perspective that is not distorted by biases, by sexism, class elitism, or internalized white supremacist thinking. When using a psychoanalytical yardstick it is evident that despite incredible economic progress and the presence of civil rights on all levels, the souls and psyches of many black Americans are troubled. Money and jobs have not made us whole, nor will they. We are sorely in need of abundant work that looks at the violence that remains at the core of the lives of many black folks in our nation. This violence, which is usually rooted in the traumatic violent aftermath of racist terror, often converges with all the other forms of violent abuse that trouble our contemporary society and its citizens. Race and racism make it more difficult to form strategies for healing that fully account for the complexity of African-American experience. Until the legacy of remembered and reenacted trauma is taken seriously, black America cannot heal.

In Judith Herman's impressive study *Trauma and Recovery*, she argues, "The knowledge of horrible events periodically intrudes into public awareness but is rarely retained for long. Denial, repression, and disassociation operate on a social as well as an individual level. The study of psychological trauma has an 'underground' history. Like traumatized people, we have been cut off from the knowledge of our past. Like traumatized people, we need to understand the past in order to reclaim the present and the future. Therefore, an understanding of psychological trauma begins with rediscovering history." For African Americans, and all who seek to understand our experience, the legacy of trauma begins with chosen exile and slavery and it continues through the years of racial apartheid and into the civil rights era. We must steadfastly work to recover and document the psychohistory of the politics of loss and abandonment that has been relentless and persistent, reenacting trauma on a collective and individual level.

When we reexamine our history we see African-American antiracist resistance move from being rooted in a love ethic and a moral philosophy centered on peace and reconciliation to a rhetoric and practice of violence. This embracing of violence as an accepted means of solving conflict and social control was an endorsement of the very politics of domination that was at the heart of antiblack racial terrorism. It has ramifications far beyond the social and political realm. It brought a socially legitimized ethos of violence into black family life. It made violence acceptable by suggesting that black men needed to be able to enact violence in order to be men. Once this way of violent thinking became more of a norm in black life, the life-affirming values that had been at the heart of antiracist struggle and constructive coping with the psychological impact of race were undermined.

The racially terroristic violence that had been traumatic during slavery did not end when slavery ended. It took a new and different form. To some extent the slaves had found constructive ways to cope with an untenable situation, similar to the prisoners of the Nazi holocaust who invented ways to nurture themselves in the midst of trauma. When slavery ended black folks were joyous, but they were also afraid and overwhelmed by renewed feelings of powerlessness, perhaps the same sensations of powerlessness they felt at the moment of enslavement. Their bodies were free but their minds were fixated on the memory of trauma and fearful of the unknown. Herman makes the point: "Psychological trauma is an affliction of the powerless. At the moment of trauma, the victim is rendered helpless by overwhelming force. When the force is that of other human beings, we speak of atrocities. Traumatic events overwhelm the ordinary systems of care that give people a sense of control, connection, and meaning."

Very few studies of Reconstruction mention the psychological aftermath of slavery. What we learn from biographies and autobiographies of this period is that folks held themselves together by focusing on material survival. In many ways a practical strategy of denial surfaced. It's as though folks intuitively understood that they did not have the structures in place for trauma recovery. They focused instead on material survival, on creating communities of resistance that gave a sense of meaning and connection and placed the welfare of the group above the individual. Black churches offered an outlet for pent-up emotions. Black music, particularly spirituals and blues, offered a vehicle for expressing feelings of loss and abandonment. Well-being and a sense of self-esteem came from the group and not from a strengthening of wounded and troubled individual black psyches.

In traditional black churches the strategies for coping with personal pain lay in giving that suffering over to a higher power, expressing one's feelings privately and in prayer. These mechanisms of coping were crucial, necessary, and they fundamentally worked. Positive group self-esteem could inadvertently impact on individual self-esteem. However, overall, until the post–civil rights era, there was little focus in black life on inner self-development. Once the patriarchally led black liberation struggle celebrated and normalized forms of violence that black survivors of racial holocaust had traditionally questioned and opposed even if they had not been able to completely eradicate them in their daily lives, black experience in America was no longer fundamentally different from white experience. Often post-slavery violence in African-American life was an imitation of the patterns of abuse utilized by the dominating white master and mistress. It was one of the first indications that black folks had internalized habits of being learned from their oppressors.

By fully embracing the values of a culture of domination,

masses of black people engaged in "splitting" (forming a frag-
mented identity). They might validate resistance to domination, exploitation, and oppression when it was based on race
but unequivocally support adult tyranny over children, gender domination of women by men, or class elitism. There is
ample historical evidence to document the growth of the
black middle class and the extent to which middle-class
blacks became enforcers of a racialized notion of personal
conduct, heaping contempt and shame on the poor and
working-class people who did not live up to their standards.
Nowadays black middle- and upper-class people continue to
use shaming to keep poor and working-class people in their
social place.

When complete racial segregation was the norm, all classes
of black folks lived in the same neighborhoods. Shaming
and patterns of exclusion and inclusion were a primary weapon of intimate terrorism, making sure that those considered
"unworthy" were kept in their place. Racial integration made
it possible for middle- and upper-class people to leave predominantly black neighborhoods, and their tyranny over the
black underclass lessened. Their flight from predominantly
black neighborhoods was in part a response to a changed economic universe where individuals who had not been born into
class privilege were gaining economic status. With money to
at least have the same standard of living as black elites, to buy
the same products, class distinctions and hierarchies were
more difficult to maintain in all black neighborhoods.

As a group, across class, most black folks who were pros-
pering in the sixties and seventies were not interested in individual therapy. Social workers "counseled" needy black folks
who were troubled. Large numbers of black people relied on
community support to cope with problems both psychologi-

cal and sociological. The black power movement of the late sixties and early seventies had made the issue of self-esteem a group concern, one that could be most effectively handled within the group. When psychiatrists such as William Grier and Price Cobbs made their pronouncements about the psyches of black folks, they relied on the same standards and judgments used by their white colleagues, adding a different perspective now and then when the issue was race. The militant call for a focus on self-esteem popularized by the "black is beautiful" aspect of antiracist struggle failed to identify racial terrorism in relationship to skin color and standards of beauty as enactments of trauma.

While it was always acknowledged that one aspect of racial terrorism was chronic sexual exploitation and abuse of black females, no one took seriously the traumatic nature of these experiences or their impact on the issue of self-esteem. Recent books that look at the way contemporary black females who are raped respond indicate how much the traumatic aspects of violation are diminished and the victims admonished to be strong and triumph over their pain. In *Surviving the Silence: Black Women's Stories of Rape* Charlotte Pierce-Baker documents the way black females, young and old, are encouraged to remain silent about rape and cope in secrecy. She writes: "There is an uncanny silence surrounding the trauma of black rape. I believe I understand the silence of black women who survive. I am a black woman wounded, and because I kept silent for so long, my newly found voice is still emerging. Silences have become important to me. I'm not sure why I refused to tell. But I do know I was intensely afraid of the truth in all its manifestations."

Throughout our history in the United States rape, both real and metaphorical, has been a ruling narrative in black female life, distorting healthy self-esteem in relation to our bodies and sexuality. Narratives of black women and rape became central themes in contemporary novels, but no one warned potential readers that they might experience secondary trauma. In the introduction to her book *Emotional Abuse,* Marti Tamm Loring writes: "It is not unusual for an individual to become retraumatized or suffer feelings of grief when reading about issues of attachment and trauma. Usually the reader will be aware of the specific experience—such as a recent loss or a past abusive incident—that has triggered the secondary trauma. At certain times, however, the incident may lie outside consciousness." In myriad ways chronic violent trauma in black American experience, of which the rape of black females is just one example, has not been seen as having residual consequences or as inducing post-traumatic stress disorder.

It is no mere accident of fate that the moment black folks began to speak more openly about the nature of their woundedness, especially through identity politics, the dominant culture began to counter this exertion of agency by introducing a sophisticated politics of blaming. More than ever before in our nation's history, conservative black folks continue to publish books and speak publicly in a discourse of discounting that seeks to counter or prove false black folks' assertion that they have been victimized by racial terrorism and racist assault and discomfort. I make this distinction because there are gradations of pain within structures of racist domination that are often not acknowledged. There is a difference between someone occasionally refusing to pick me up in a cab because of my skin color and systematic refusal of equal rights based on race.

There is a direct correspondence between reenactment of

trauma and troubled self-esteem. Until we acknowledge this fact conservatives will continue to look for ways to blame folks who are victimized. At one point in our history black folks, irrespective of whether they were conservative or liberal, validated the pain expressed by victims of racial terrorism or racial assault. Nowadays many of the individual black folks who write work that calls attention to self-sabotage do so not to show the reasons many black folks have internalized faulty logic but rather to blame them or to discount the idea that any of us are ever really victims. This is similar to the contemporary individuals who, despite monumental evidence that proves them wrong, claim that Jews were not brutally slaughtered in the Nazi holocaust.

Black woman writer Toni Cade Bambara, a participant in militant antiracist black power struggle, writes in "Deep Sighting and Rescue Missions" a useful retrospective insight that "critical monitoring of process is necessary in order to overcome the powerful pull domination and demonizing exert in this society."

For so many years black people lived in fear of racist white folks imposing demonizing stereotypes aimed at silencing any attempt to name the pain of racism and demand accountability. Now they must face fellow African Americans who mock and ridicule their articulations of pain, who are quick to insist that the claims of other black folks to victimization are fraudulent. These individuals never consider that post-traumatic stress could be a factor influencing an individual to overreact in incidents where observers who know nothing of that person's psychological history may see the situation in an utterly different light. For example: An individual who was beaten as a child because it was assumed that dark skin meant that he was bad or evil might respond in an ambivalent or anxious manner whenever anyone makes a comment about his skin color, even if what was said is positive. Any statement about his skin might trigger stress and lead to a hypervigilant negative response.

Individual black thinkers, most of whom are conservative, seek to discount and diminish the pain of fellow black folks who want not only to speak their anguish (whether they are claiming to be victims or not) but also to raise questions about accountability. They attempt to shame these folks by mockingly labeling them "victimologists." Since they refuse to connect the continued successful perpetuation of racism and white supremacy with the chronic reenactment of trauma, they rely more on facts, data, and statistics than on psychological interpretations. Unwittingly they reproduce, albeit in a slightly different way, racist logic. The harshness with which they judge black peers often is contrasted with a keen willingness to extend to white folks a more generous and compassionate critical evaluation. This harshness is itself a reflection of a racist climate wherein it is deemed acceptable by society to be more judgmental of the actions of black folks, who are often held to higher standards and who are then found wanting.

Increasingly, social critics tell us that self-sabotage in black life is not the result of racism, but rarely do they explore with any degree of profundity the complex circumstances all blacks face in white supremacist, capitalist patriarchy. Most of this work is done by thinkers who are biased by patriarchal perspectives, which is why so much of it reinforces the notion that individual willpower is all that is needed to overcome oppression and exploitation, and issues of self-esteem are regarded as unimportant. Indeed, this failure to see the importance of self-esteem is a reflection of mainstream culture's disinterest in the issue of self-esteem.

To gain optimal benefit from racial integration, black folks were compelled to surrender the oppositional subcultural values developed in a segregated context that often shielded the black psyche from the assaults that had been commonplace in the culture of whiteness. Since white culture normalized violence, militant black male leaders were correct in assuming that black folks would assimilate better if the ethos of violence was at the center of our lives. Embracing this ethos, black people were placed in adversarial relationship to ourselves. We became the enemies of our own self-esteem, both collective and individual. Gaining equality within white supremacist capitalist patriarchy, black folks did not vigilantly create strategies to maintain high levels of self-regard. Bambara cautions us to remember that: "We often overestimate the degree to which exploitative behavior has been normalized and the degree to which we've internalized these norms. It takes, then, a commitment to an acutely self-conscious practice to be able to think and behave better than we've been taught."

There was no acutely self-conscious programmatic practice ushered in by contemporary black liberation. For example: There was no essay or pamphlet written that addressed the psychological impact on the minds of black children of being taught by teachers who embodied white supremacist thinking. No one wrote about the steps black folks would need to take to create and maintain healthy self-esteem while integrating and, to some extent, assimilating.

Of course even before racial integration had become the norm, television was the medium used to colonize the black mind, socializing black folks to passively accept white supremacist thinking. By watching television, black folks who were not critical viewers were indoctrinated by passively absorbing the values of the dominant white culture. Those values were reinforced by a racially integrated educational structure whose values and principles were grounded in the logic of white supremacy. No wonder, then, that the critical vigilance that had been deployed historically by black folks to create a subculture of resistance, of oppositional values, was diminished. As masses of black folks passively accepted the values of white supremacist, capitalist patriarchy, allowing their minds and their imaginations to be colonized, they were placed in an adversarial relationship with themselves.

Unwittingly, many black folks began to deprive themselves of access to the very systems of progressive thought that would enable them to create healthy self-esteem. That deprivation is the reason why the issue of self-esteem has been deemed unimportant. In actuality, the problems facing black America will never be solved without a widespread effort to establish mental health care communities wherein folks can learn how to create healthy self-esteem.

3

Ending the Shame That Binds

Long before black-skinned bodies arrived on the shores of the New World, whether as free individuals (that is, the folks who came from Africa before Columbus and the folks who later immigrated to the Americas of their own choosing for the same reasons white settlers came) or as an enslaved group, racist iconography had dubbed black bodies marked by a biblical curse. The identifiable dark skin was considered by white Christians the mark of shame that singled out these groups to be subordinated, to serve those superior "white" bodies who were chosen. This is a vital observation, as it allows us to remember that even before there was contact between the races there were negative assumptions made and stereotypes formed in the minds and imaginations of white folks. An emotional pornography had been created that was borne out in Europe when images of black bodies as well as live individual naked black bodies were paraded at parties for the entertainment of self-proclaimed civilized white people.

A system of shaming was then already in place within the white European mindset before white folks actually encountered black folks on an everyday basis. Mocking, ridiculing, and labeling black bodies as animalistic were all the ways a system of psychological terrorism was put in place before actual interracial contact. White colonizers encountering Africans during the slave trade were ready to enact shaming as a strategy of colonization. Paul Taylor comments on the deeper implications of this shaming in his essay "Malcolm's Conk and Danto's Colors":

> The most prominent type of racialist thought took shape under the same intellectual circum-stances that in the eighteenth century produced efforts to define an aesthetic morality centered on "the beautiful soul" and in the nineteenth century led to the "science" of physiognomy . . . the widespread assumption that bodily beauty and deformity covary with moral beauty and deformity as well as with general cultural and intellectual capacity. This practice of conflating different cate-gories of value—of running together the good, the beautiful, the intelligent, and the civilized—could only have made it easier for hierarchical racialism to become what I call thick racialism, which holds that the physical differences between races are signs of deeper, typically intellectual and moral, differ-ences. Thus it became part of the content of the standard thick, hierarchical racialism—what I call classical racialism—that the physical ugliness of black people was a sign of a deeper ugliness and depravity.

Thick or thin, this racialism became the ideology that sup-ported the brutal dehumanization of black folks on the basis of skin color.

Shaming is one way to intimidate and break the spirit. Enslaved Africans were an easy target. Already trapped in the trauma and indignity of the middle passage, fearing death, enslaved black folks were primed by the horribleness of their experience to acquiesce and submit.

Naked on auction blocks in a world far different from their familiar understandings, joined with other darker-skinned folks who did not necessarily speak the same language, enslaved black people were vulnerable to shaming. As they assimilated and conformed to the customs of life in the Americas they were also taught religious beliefs that reinforced shaming. In *Coming Out of Shame* therapists Gershen Kaufman and Lev Raphael write:

> Shame is a deeply disturbing human emotion that becomes triggered anew throughout the life cycle, from birth to death. Shame is by no means confined to just one time of life. During each successive, unfolding phase of development, from childhood and adolescence to adulthood and old age, there are distinctive sources of shame. It is ever-present in our lives, however masked it may be. This perplexing emotion is also passed from each generation to the next; the transfer is mediated directly by critical scenes of shame which become internalized through imagery but which then are reactive and reenacted with others.

The most obvious internalization of shame that impacted on the self-esteem of black folks historically and continues to the present day is the shame about appearance, skin color, body shape, and hair texture. Had white colonizers chosen to exploit and oppress black people without stigmatizing appearance, the psychological trauma endured by the slaves would not continue to reenact itself in similar forms today.

We will never know when enslaved black folks began to understand fully that the more they imitated the mores of their white colonizers the better they might be treated. We will never recall that exact moment in time when a significant number of dark-skinned enslaved Africans began to see lighter skin as better. A color caste system existed in the minds of white colonizers long before the systematic rape of black women produced children with mixed skin color. It may have been as simple a transition as slaves observing that white folks treated lighter-skinned people better, and ultimately this began to establish a new standard of aesthetics based primarily on the longing to be treated with less brutality.

Significantly, biblical metaphors of color that likened darkness to evil and fairness to good were a prime source of brainwashing legitimizing color caste. Religious teachings, preferential treatment given fair-skinned black folks, the ease with which one could comb and attend to straightened hair over kinky hair, all were factors that together induced passive acceptance of a color caste hierarchy. Most black Americans, from slavery to the present day, along with white Americans and other nonblack folks, have passively accepted and condoned color caste. Shaming on the basis of skin color is one racially based trauma retention that has been passed on from generation to generation.

Of course when all black people were dark skinned, shaming each other on the basis of skin color would not have had much significance. Since biracial children were the production of violent rape, it may very well be that the black females who bore these children were initially revolted by their appearance. Overvaluation of light-skinned children may have been the strategy needed to draw them into the group. However, it is the privileging of lighter-skinned folks, emerging from the rape of black women by white men, that leads to the institutionalization of a color caste system. Whites and lighter-skinned biracial mixtures, as well as their offspring who mated with whites and blacks, produced a diversity of color. These lighter groups, internalizing the aesthetic and moral values of their white colonizers more often than not, embraced a color caste system that gave them a higher standard than that of dark-skinned blacks.

Long after slavery ended, a more privileged class of black folks who were fairer skinned participated in creating and sustaining hierarchical social arrangements where they lorded it over their darker counterparts. Since they often lacked concrete material privilege, skin color itself became the mark of status. Like the racist white master and mistress, a fair-skinned black person could deploy shaming on the basis of color to ridicule and treat with contempt darker folk. Naturally, individual dark-skinned black folks rebelled against this internalization of racist thinking, but their rebellion did not win the day.

Significantly, the same white supremacist thinking that led to the formation of color castes in black American life also included the notion that the brains of black folks were smaller than the brains of white folks, and that this made us the inferior race. Black folks utterly rebelled against this notion. It was not internalized during slavery. And the great majority of black folks saw themselves as victims of unfortunate circumstance, believing that if they had the same opportunity as their white counterparts they would demonstrate intellectual equality. Perversely, black folks who passively accepted the internalization of the color caste system wholeheartedly resisted the notion that they were inferior based on intellectual capability.

One mode of colonizing thought referred to outward appearance, which though important was not considered as crucial as the state of the mind and spirit in nineteenth-century life. Appearance, coming under the issue of aesthetics, was linked to the idea of beauty as well as desire. No doubt plenty of black males, aping the manners and mores of their white masters, desired lighter-skinned females, and that desire influenced their willingness to accept hierarchies based on color. When similar white supremacist logic was applied to the issue of intellectual capability, black males were not willing to passively absorb white supremacist logic and perpetuate it. They consistently opposed any racist who insisted that black men were intellectually inferior to white men. Similarly, black women who were the mothers of these fairer-skinned children who were more likely than darker counterparts to garner favor were competitive with mothers who produced darker offspring, wanting their child to be the recipient of special favors and privileges (especially if those favors kept a family united or lessened work and brutal treatment). Like colonized black men, the black women who endorsed color caste resisted the notion that there was a hierarchy of the intellect in which darker-skinned folks were deemed inferior.

Engaging in a form of psychological splitting, black folks could resist racist thinking that suggested they were the intellectual inferiors of whites while not only accepting but perpetuating the notion that fairer skin made one more valuable. This splitting continued to take place in African-American life. It led to a convergence of the two categories; since fairer-skinned people usually had greater access to privileges they were more likely to gain access to various resources, especially education, that enabled them to improve their lot with much greater ease than their darker counterparts. Visit any predominantly black college in the United States and examine a photo-history of its pupils from the institution's inception to the present day and one will see a visual collage of skin color politics. In most cases pictures of female students will show how "white" everyone looked. As fair-skinned black people were usually among the privileged, they happily continued their reign over darker-skinned black folks. Their color caste tyranny, like that of the white colonizer, was advanced by the politics of shame.

Racial apartheid has shaped and continues to shape the intimate lives of citizens in the United States. Most black people spend their personal social time primarily with other black people. The same is true for whites and other nonblack groups. Within all of these groups some form of color caste system exists, for example, whites valuing blond, blue-eyed people more, seeing them as the epitome of beauty, or different Asian groups overvaluing fair skin. Tragically, in the midst of state-legitimized racial apartheid, in predominantly black communities everywhere, the intimate terrorism of the color caste is enacted. Children are its most vulnerable victims.

In my first women's studies class, when contemporary feminist movement was just starting, I was the only black female. The white students did not comprehend what I was talking about when I disagreed with their assumption that at the moment of an infant's birth (when it exits the maternal body), the first concern is the child's gender identity. I shared with them that in black American life when a newborn is emerging from the body what is first noticed is skin

ʟack parents know skin color will, to a grave
determine some aspects of their child's destiny
.s gender.

f the most perverse ironies of white supremacy is the
way in which white colonizers created skin-color castes that
were kept in place by white folks who, within their group, val-
ued fair skin over darker complexions, straight hair over curly,
and yet who adamantly disavowed any knowledge of white
supremacist thinking when it came to aesthetics. Time and
time again I have seen white folks recoil when hearing about
the brutal dimensions of color caste hierarchies as they are
played out in black life, who, however, see no connection
between their aesthetics and the colonized black person's worship of whiteness.

All black people have witnessed someone being victimized
by the politics of color, whether it's hearing slogans like "a
black nigger is a no-good nigger" or watching an adult degrade a child by suggesting he is evil because he is so black, or
by hearing a child speak contemptuously to another child
about her appearance. Every day somewhere in our culture a
child is telling another child: "I can't play with you because
you are too dark." Or, "You can't come to my party 'cause your
hair is too nappy." My maternal grandmother, who was able
to pass for white, always degraded our darker-skinned sister,
calling her "Blackie." As children we witnessed my sister's
wounds, the ways they affected her self-worth, and we felt
fearful for our own self-worth.

I shall never forget the ebullient feelings that surfaced in our
household when militant antiracist black power movement
offered us a liberatory counternarrative by celebrating the
beauty of blackness. This call for self-acceptance laid the foundation for a psychological revolution by emphasizing the

struggle, true freedom would not be possible until the minds and imaginations of black folks were decolonized. Essentially this process could not happen without a focus on mental health and without a psychology of resistance. That psychology was not in place. Even though black psychiatrists and psychologists contributed to liberation struggle by describing the ways the self-esteem of black folks was damaged by racism, they did not lead the way to freedom by offering mental health strategies aimed at decolonization. They did not remind black folks that efforts to decolonize their minds would be an even longer, more protracted struggle, requiring critical vigilance, than the fight for civil rights.

This critical vigilance was particularly needed in regard to the way attitudes about the black body and beauty were so fundamentally shaped by white supremacist thinking. Progressive black folks created an amazing body of work during the late sixties and early seventies on the issues of race and racism. Yet that work barely addressed the issue of self-esteem and the prolonged psychological trauma inflicted by shaming about skin color and the body. In part these areas were ignored because much of the progressive writing of this period was done by black men. And even though black males were victimized by color caste hierarchies, it was possible for dark-skinned black men to transcend the limitations of color in ways that were not in place for black females. Ultimately, sexist thinking about the body meant that everyone placed more value on female appearance than on the appearance of males. Since black women, like all women in this culture, were the primary parental caretakers, black males could easily remain unconscious of the impact of color caste on children. They could notice color but still deny that it was important. Leaders like Martin Luther King, Jr., could talk and write about love without ever mentioning black self-esteem. Malcolm X was a heroic figure to so many young black folks during his lifetime precisely because he addressed the issue of self-esteem. Overall, however, black male political leaders were struggling to challenge job discrimination and the criminalization of black manhood, issues they saw as "hard," and the color caste system was viewed as a "soft" issue. This was just one of the many instances in black liberation struggle where patriarchal thinking created a fatal blind spot.

Many black folks remained psychologically stuck in internalized shame about skin color, hair texture, and the overall black body, unable to acquire the necessary self-regard to develop healthy self-esteem. Although the color caste system was not eliminated collectively by black folks, it was consistently challenged on an individual level. Shame about the black body did not necessarily keep some black folks from succeeding in careers. Often brutal shaming was the catalyst for black people deemed "inferior" or "bad" by other black folks because of their skin color to work hard and excel to prove their goodness and worth. The underlying low self-esteem about the body easily remained constant and invariably became the catalyst for self-sabotage.

Low self-esteem rooted in negative perceptions of blackness was reinforced by mass media, especially television. Black folks who appeared on our screens were either chosen because they embodied racist stereotypes (e.g. images of black servants) or because they reflected a beauty informed by color caste (Dorothy Dandridge set the standard). The beautiful "good" black women who appeared on our television screens were always light-skinned females with straight hair. The "ugly" black female was either a faithful servant or a villain. The television movie *Introducing Dorothy Dandridge* created a fictive world where all the black villains were dark skinned and all the good people fair skinned or white.

When television screens had only rare images of black folks, black people were more critically vigilant about these representations. Even when blackness was represented "positively," as it was in early black television shows like *Julia,* which focused on the life of a black nurse, the beauty standard was a reflection of white supremacist aesthetics. When black folks made the first films featuring all-black casts they relied on the familiar color-based stereotypes and standards when it came to the casting of female characters. This pattern has continued. Films made today by filmmakers of all races and particularly those by black filmmakers continue to reinforce white supremacist aesthetics.

The black female body is the site where white supremacist thinking about beauty and blackness is reinscribed again and again. Dark-skinned black males, though often portrayed stereotypically, play a number of roles in mass media. They are not always and only villains. They are not always and only depicted as ugly, or less than desirable. Yet whether the images are those of black girls or black women, the color caste is in place and dictates the standards. The contemporary movie *Soul Food* depicts images of three black sisters, all of whom are fair skinned with straight hair, all of whom are portrayed as desirable. Their black male partners are different colors—one is dark, one is light, one is brown skinned—but they are all depicted as desirable. The only darker-skinned black female character is the obese brown-skinned mama; she is not portrayed as desirable. These racist, sexist stereotypes are all-pervasive. They set the standards in all mass media. Yet scholars and writers who work on the subject of race have not created a progressive body of work that examines fully the connection between shaming about the black body and low self-esteem. It continues to be the case that the most brutal stigma of color affects females more than males.

Since sexism leads men to be judged more by how they perform than by how they appear, the black male who may feel wounded and shamed by color stigmas may feel he can triumph over those stigmas. Michael Jordan's success is a prime example. His dark black body is deemed beautiful both here in the United States and globally. Yet there is no dark-skinned black female who occupies a similar position. Even though there are still only a few successful black models, and among that few are some very dark-skinned females, only the ones who have straight hair, whether wigs or natural hair, get to go to the top of the charts. In the world of fashion dark bodies are portrayed as "exotica" but never as naturally beautiful. In the world of television there is no black female star who holds center stage who has a natural hairdo. Even the high priestess of black self-help Iyanla Vanzant stopped wearing her hair natural when she made it to television. She came to her success preaching self-love and self-esteem, using her own life as an example of how black folks can start at the bottom and rise. But when it comes to the representation of beauty, black females can only rise so far. The standard again is different for black men. Most successful black males wear their hair naturally. Even though black men have always participated to some extent in the chemical straightening of hair, those males were always a minority.

In black youth culture white supremacist aesthetics prevail. Yet they are given their most graphic expression in representations of the black female. While black male rappers create antiracist lyrics that project critical consciousness, that consciousness stops when it comes to the black female body.

More than any other propagandistic tool, television shows that focus on black youth reinscribe white supremacist aesthetics with a vengeance. Dark-skinned females are rarely depicted at all. And even light-skinned black females get no play unless they have long straight hair. Speaking about her career as a rapper in *Essence,* the magazine for "Today's Black Woman," Lil' Kim acknowledges: "When I was younger all the men liked the same women: those light-skinned European-looking girls. Being the rapper Lil' Kim has helped me to deal with it a little better because I get to dress up in expensive clothes and look like a movie star. All the people responding to me has helped. Because I still don't see what they see." The more Lil' Kim distorted her natural beauty to become a cartoonlike caricature of whiteness, the larger her success. Donning blond wigs and getting a boob job so that she can resemble a cheap version of the white womanhood she adores wins her monetary success in the world of white supremacist, patriarchal capitalism and helps her cover up the fact that she has no self-worth. She testifies that creating a "false self" in the persona of Lil' Kim, the personification of a childlike ho, bolsters her low self-esteem. To her credit she does not pretend that it makes the low self-esteem go away, it just helps her cope. And this is a young woman whom thousands upon thousands of black girls want to emulate.

Television remains the most accessible mass medium. Many folks can just barely read or do not read at all, and books and magazines are not cheap. Folks look to television to learn how to think and feel about themselves and about their skin color. Television narratives perpetuate color caste. The color caste system has been most exposed and interrogated in the fiction written by black female authors. Contemporary black women novelists have written the stories that most vividly chronicle the pain and anguish of internalized low self-esteem rooted in shame about the body. From acclaimed writer Gwendolyn Brooks's groundbreaking novel on the issue of color, *Maud Martha*, to Toni Morrison's *The Bluest Eye*, the nature of crippling low self-esteem based on color is talked about. Morrison's fictional little black girl Pecola wants blue eyes because she feels that they will give her a better life.

Morrison was one of the first black women novelists to critique the concept of physical beauty. In *The Bluest Eye* she writes that the concept of beauty is one of "the most destructive ideas in the history of human thought." Writing about an adult black female character's self-esteem, she tells readers: "She was never able, after her education in the movies, to look at a face and not assign it some category in the scale of absolute beauty, and the scale was one she absorbed in full from the silver screen." A dangerous form of psychological splitting had to have taken place, and it continues to take place, in the psyches of many African Americans who can on one hand oppose racism, and then on the other hand passively absorb ways of thinking about beauty that are rooted in white supremacist thought.

The normalization of this dysfunction has had disastrous consquences for the self-esteem of many African Americans. Every day that African Americans partake of mainstream mass media, in particular visual media, we are subjected to covert and overt representations of an aesthetic informed by white supremacist thinking. Without constant critical vigilance we are all likely to succumb to the seduction of images that basically teach us that all things fair are better than all things dark. Subliminal suggestion acts upon us even when there is no open discourse about race or racism. When black folks look at the movie *Soul Food*, no one in the film ever mentions skin color, but the color caste system is perpetuated by the choice of females depicted as desirable.

Children are willing to identify and openly assert their received understanding that black is bad and white is good. Studies still show that children, including black children, prefer white dolls to black dolls. Every day in our nation thousands of black children are asking parents to change them in some way so that they can be more like white peers. They know from watching television that everything white is better.

A few years ago a children's book by black author Carolivia Herron was published called *Nappy Hair*. Reproducing an aspect of traditional black folk culture called "signifying," the story tells of a little dark-skinned girl who is continually mocked for having nappy hair. In the end she is portrayed as triumphing over this mocking. The images accompanying the text are ugly. Portrayed as grotesque and unfeminine (there is nothing girl-like about the cartoon stick figure), she could be a strange-looking boy, an animal. When first published this book was not a success. Yet when an attractive young white schoolteacher claimed that black parents had threatened her for reading the book to little black children, it made national news. Her image was everywhere in magazines and on television. Suddenly the book was a success. No one wrote about the reasons black parents, mostly poor and working-class folk, opposed the teaching of this book. When I was critical of this work, calling attention to the way it reproduces shaming, white peers pointed out to me that it was written by a black woman. They show surprise when I emphasize that black folks have internalized white supremacist thought. Colonized grown black people are the group that emotionally abuse black children by shaming them about their bodies daily.

Many adult black folks who do not believe in their heart of hearts that white is better feel they must "wear the mask" to get ahead in jobs and careers. Wearing the mask may include straightening one's hair so that unenlightened white folks, particularly prospective employers or other authority figures, will feel more comfortable. When I wear my hair in braids I find I am often perceived to be a threat, or undesirable, when encountering the unenlightened white public. That same public regards me more positively when my hair appears straightened. Lots of white folks have learned to associate black folks and natural hair with race pride. The logic of white supremacy equates loving blackness with being antiwhite. As a consequence, black folks who choose to love themselves may appear to most white folks as threats.

Until these white folks collectively decolonize their minds they send the message to black folks that "we are more comfortable when you look, talk, and act like us." All black folks are pressured to assimilate. Imitating the look of white folks by straightening hair and coloring one's hair blond may increase a black person's value in the eyes of white colonizers. Even though more black folks than ever before choose to wear natural hair, very few powerful public figures or successful entertainers who are black and female are able to wear their hair in its natural state.

Even though black male bodies, of all shades and hues, are deemed attractive and desirable by mainstream media, especially because of the positive representation of these bodies in sports, black men still feel shame about skin color. Significantly, as the black male body began to be represented positively in popular culture, especially in the world of advertising, that body was and is hypersexualized. This modern reconfiguration of the black male as sexual predator in no way differs from the negative racist stereotypes that prevailed in the nineteenth century and early twentieth century. The difference is that the idea of the black male as inherently a bestial sexual predator is now often portrayed as "cool" and the dehumanizing nature of this construction is obscured. And of course there is little work done on the waning self-esteem of black males that connects the two issues. Overall, black males have responded with collusion and passivity to the resurgence of these stereotypes.

In all the cases where acceptance of color caste and denigration of the black body has meant more employment or even the acquisition of wealth, black folks tend to minimize the psychological impact. Aware black actors who play roles in media that correspond to degrading negative stereotypes may recognize the hypocrisy of their actions. They may see that these roles may reinforce racism and white supremacy, but they justify their actions by arguing that this is what they must do to be paid.

Like many concerned antiracist activists I have pondered why black people in general have gained a measure of equality within our existing social system and yet these gains have had so little impact on our collective self-esteem. When we examine the issue of self-acceptance as a crucial component of self-esteem, it is evident that shaming about the black body continues to be a norm and assaults the sensibilities of black folks from all walks of life. Talented, economically successful black folks often have low self-esteem in relation to their bodies, and their disadvantaged poor peers may suffer from the same malaise. This low self-esteem may lead them to self-sabotage in areas where they may have all the skills to excel.

To change the effects of low self-esteem related to body image, representations of blackness must change on all levels in our society. And in those instances where we cannot change representations, we need to be critically vigilant, exercising our right to boycott products, to turn off our television sets, to send magazines back to publishers. Imagine how different black life would be if so many of us did not passively consume television. Before I knew about the existence of the book *Nappy Hair,* I wrote and sold a children's book called *Happy to Be Nappy.* My intent was not to follow the usual routine of books marketed to black children and write the usual story that tells them how bad they are but that they should love themselves. The self-esteem of black children is threatened when a children's book that suggests you can mock, ridicule, and shame black children and they will triumph in the end is designated positive. This is dangerous propaganda rooted in faulty logic. All black folks risk being victimized by the perpetuation of the notion that we can triumph with ease over degradation and dehumanization.

Conservative separatist black nationalists have been and continue to be the group that most identify self-esteem as a political issue. Yet their work is often biased by patriarchal and fundamentalist religious thought. Since we live in an integrated society, it's essential that black folks cultivate self-esteem that is sustained in both predominantly black and nonblack settings. The culture of white supremacist capitalist patriarchy assaults black self-esteem. However, there are many strategies black folks can use to resist these assaults. When we decolonize our minds, we can maintain healthy self-esteem despite the racism and white supremacy that surround us.

4

Living with Integrity

Developing the capacity to mask feelings and lie was a useful survival skill for black folks during slavery and during the brutal apartheid years of Reconstruction and Jim Crow. During the civil rights era and militant black power struggle individual leaders emphasized the importance of black folks' standing up for their rights and confronting white racism. Yet for most black folks the inherited legacy of simulating submission and never showing feelings, especially to white folks, was not unlearned, particularly in the southern states. To this day in the south, as vast numbers of black people rank among the economically and educationally disenfranchised, the same patterns of submission that were aspects of slavery surface. Fear of white scorn and retaliation makes it impossible for many black folks to speak freely to white folks.

In an integrated society with full civil rights, utilizing outmoded survival strategies actually creates dysfunction in social relations. Masking true feelings and lying, whether in the public sphere (which is the place where black people most interface with white folks) or in private lives, creates a lack of communication and understanding. The normalization of lying as a survival strategy did not stop with the white master and mistress; it was deployed in black-on-black social relations.

A central aspect of self-esteem is the capacity to be a person of integrity. In *Six Pillars of Self-Esteem* Nathaniel Branden offers this clear, succinct definition: "Integrity is the integration of ideals, convictions, standards, beliefs—and behavior. When our behavior is congruent with our professed values, when ideals and practice match, we have integrity." Enlightened elderly black folks in the apartheid south, many of them the direct descendants of slaves, recognized that to decolonize their minds they needed to both challenge white racist stereotypes, which claimed black folks were incapable of honesty, and challenge as well themselves and black peers because they had all learned the survival strategy of being duplicitous to circumvent exploitation and oppression. To these elders the practice of integrity was crucial. My maternal grandparents preached regular sermons to my siblings and me about the importance of being people of our word. My mother's mother was fond of repeatedly stating in her business deals and transactions, "My word is my bond." And many is the time she told me, "Little girl, you are only ever as good as your word." In the community we lived in it was important to be known as a person who was forthright, honest, and in all ways able to act with integrity.

In his insightful book *Integrity,* Stephen Carter explains that integrity means more than simply being honest because it requires the capacity to act with discernment, to have the "sustained moral reflection that is often needed to tell right from wrong." He makes the point that one cannot have integrity without being honest, but one can be honest and yet have little integrity. Carter sees integrity as having three steps of moral reflection, "discerning what is right and what is wrong, acting on what you have discerned, even at personal cost, and saying openly that you are acting on your understanding of right from wrong."

To understand why many African Americans shifted their ethical values away from the ethos of acting with integrity back to the defensive strategy of lying in order to acquire an advantage in the interest of survival, we must acknowledge that the values our ethical elders promoted were not those encouraged by mainstream white supremacist capitalist society. When many black Americans measured their potential for freedom, success, and well-being against the standard set by white middle-class culture and the burgeoning culture of class privilege that prioritized consumerism and greed, they saw ethical and moral values as impediments.

By the late sixties most black folks did not consider that a central aspect of self-esteem was the practice of personal integrity. Young patriarchal militant black male leaders had told them it was fine to lie, cheat, and steal to get over on the all-powerful white men whom they insisted had broken all the laws of human decency in order to dominate and rule in the first place. When despairing black citizens begin to see the continued racial strife in the United States as a war without end, they begin to capitulate to the prevailing social order, abandoning the notion that it is important to emotional well-being to maintain high moral standards.

To win over "the man" one had to get down on his level. The vulgarization of Malcolm X's mandate that black folk attain freedom "by any means necessary" was a call to abandon living consciously and with integrity. The betrayal of our nation's ideals of freedom and democracy signified by the refusal of state and government to truly end discrimination in jobs, housing, and education shattered the fragile hope of many black folks who had once believed in the values taught them but who then saw those values disregarded by those in power. The assassination of liberal and progressive leaders was the painful exposure of that betrayal. The loss of civic trust, broken by promises that were not kept by our nation's leaders and white citizens, led many black folk, especially the economically and culturally disenfranchised, to uphold corruption and lawlessness.

The civil rights and black power generation of black folks differed from their predecessors in that we were not as familiar with white folks. We had not had the intimate contact with whiteness that was the norm for generations of black folks who had worked as servants in white homes. And to some extent not knowing them led many of this new generation of black folks to create an idealized portrait of whiteness. By the early fifties television also offered an idealized portrait of white family life. The white folks we watched on our television screens were usually depicted as kind, honest, loyal, ethical, and capable of acting with integrity.

Racial desegregation and integration created a context where fantasies were disrupted by a real world of whiteness. As in the past, working with and among "real" white folks, this new generation of black folks saw the underbelly of whiteness. They saw more white people who were dishonest, cruel, and licentious profit from wrongdoing and rarely encountered an ethical white person. Often the white folks black workers encountered were among the most corrupt. Branden states: "If we live in a society where business associates, corporate heads, political figures, religious leaders, and other public personalities hold themselves to high standards of morality, it is relatively easier for an average person to practice integrity than in a society where corruption, cynicism, and amorality are the norm. In the latter kind of society, the individual is likely to feel that the quest for personal integrity is futile and unrealistic." This sense of the futility of maintaining personal integrity is widespread in American life and certainly pervasive in the lives of black folks.

To many black people corruption appeared to be the American way. Lorraine Hansberry dramatized this conflict in her prophetic, award-winning 1959 play *A Raisin in the Sun*. When Lena Younger, the ethical mother who promotes non-market values, asks her son Walter Lee the question, "Since when did money become life?" he answers, "It was always life, Mama, but we just did not know it." According to Walter Lee white people had always known that to be corrupt was the only way to get ahead. He saw black folk as clinging to outmoded moral and ethical values. To him black people needed to learn how to be ruthless, how to sacrifice the good of the group for the individual in order to make it in America. In Hansberry's drama ethical values win the day. Walter Lee's shaky sense of self-esteem is bolstered when he makes the responsible choice. He becomes a man of integrity who can assume full responsibility for the care and protection of his family.

Tragically, masses of young black folks were already moving away from the values praised by Lena Younger, the values she and her deceased hardworking husband of years endeavored to instill in their children: a work ethic and a love ethic. This was the generation of black children who were the product of integrated schools and affirmative action benefits, which have enabled members of poor and working-class groups to attend predominantly white colleges. From the late sixties into the eighties before affirmative action backlash, this new generation of black folks composed of both those who had decolonized our minds and those of us who were more than willing to remain colonized and assimilate or pretend to assimilate to make it big-time in the mainstream had a genuine crisis of values.

Those of us who decolonized our minds were attempting to follow the revolutionary constructive oppositional values of our ancestors yet still develop the skills needed to succeed in the existing social order. And a great many of us were trying to play the game, to appear to be assimilating while maintaining different values away from work or any social interaction with white people. Then there were the conservative thinkers among us who believed deeply that the best strategy for success was to embrace liberal individualism, to eschew signs of "black culture" and act as much like one's white counterparts as possible. All of these choices create new psychological stresses, and yet their presence in our lives did not lead to the cultivation of mental care aimed at addressing the issues.

A primary issue that was never addressed was the shaming and other forms of emotional abuse many of us experienced in higher education as we endeavored to relate to and please authority figures, of all races but mostly white, who had not divested themselves of racist thinking and practice. These encounters assaulted our self-esteem. Those of us who were coming from segregated black worlds into a culture dominated by white people, the vast majority of whom had not divested themselves of white supremacist thinking, often drove ourselves crazy trying to balance the two worlds. In one world we had been taught that the good of the group was paramount; in the other world we were being taught the primacy of individual will and the individual drive to succeed.

A crisis of values led many black folks coming out of these experiences to behave in ways that created intense inner turmoil and conflict. Writing about the practice of personal integrity, Branden states, "When we behave in ways that conflict with our judgment of what is appropriate, we lose face in our own eyes. We respect ourselves less. If the policy becomes habitual, we trust ourselves less or cease to trust ourselves at all." Significantly, Branden writes that the practice of personal integrity usually requires us to ask the questions: "Am I honest, reliable, and trustworthy? Do I keep my promises? Do I do the things I say I admire and do I avoid the things I say I deplore? Am I fair and just in my dealings with others?" Inner turmoil over issues of personal integrity has intensified among black people of all classes as the ethics of greed have become a norm in our society.

To a grave extent many of the black folks who have retreated into an idealized utopian vision of blackness have done so to avoid having to cope with conflicting values and standards. All over our nation the rise in fundamentalist thinking corresponds with a feeling that many people have that they no longer know how to judge right and wrong. Those feelings are often intensified in the lives of people of color, and black people particularly. For example: Consider the poor single mother who is raising her children in a housing project, barely able to make ends meet. She has taught her children ethical values. She is antiviolence, antidrugs. She has a teenage son who begins to bring money into the home from selling drugs. She knows his actions are ethically and morally wrong, but she is conflicted about the appropriate way to respond. Another example coming from my experience: Imagine an extremely bright young black girl raised in the dorms of a prestigious college by a hardworking college-educated single mom. She is in charge of dorm life, has taught her child ethical and moral values. As she grows up, the girl hangs out with mostly white friends who are also gifted and bright but who come from economically privileged backgrounds. Even though the girl has had most of her material needs met she wants to be an equal with her peers. She begins to steal to gain material advantage. She knows her actions are wrong, yet she also holds the competing belief that anything goes if it gets you what you want. Motivated by deep-seated resentments of her race and class, her acting out exposes the crippling low self-esteem that emerged when she began to understand the differences separating her life circumstances and those of her peers. Sadly, her actions create stress for both her mom and herself. And the mental health of both suffers.

For far too long African Americans have held to the belief that we might have shady dealings in the world of whiteness, but when we return to the segregated worlds of blackness our integrity can be intact. This is simply not the case. The world of blackness has become just as corrupt as the world of whiteness. The impact of lying and betrayal in black-on-black social relations is dire. In fact many folks who first idealized whiteness only to find that fantasy disrupted turn to blackness looking for an alternative and are even more shattered when they find there the same evils they had to contend with in the white world.

Certainly, any examination of the estrangement between heterosexual black women and men in intimate relationships reveals the role lying and deceit plays in undermining trust. Without trust there can be no love. Lying damages self-esteem. While the black male "player," a man who womanizes, is often depicted positively in film and literature, his whole life revolves around the betrayal of himself and others. The same is true of his female counterpart. Even though sexism in African-American life makes her actions more reprehensible than those of her male counterpart, the truth is that both individuals deprive themselves of the personal integrity essential for well-being. Sex-addict behavior is usually the drug used to fill the void of moral emptiness. Emotional pain can be covered up when one is running from one liaison to another.

As children witnessing our father's lies about womanizing, we learn to recognize adult hypocrisy. Branden reminds us in *Six Pillars of Self-Esteem* that "Hypocrisy, by its very nature, is self-invalidating. It is mind rejecting itself. A default on integrity undermines me and contaminates my sense of self." Our society has made it seem that to lie and cheat is acceptable behavior. Studies show that Americans lie when it would be simpler to tell the truth. The most devastating indictment of this cultural trend is the way more and more children lie constantly to cope with any situation where they are called upon to act with moral discernment. When children risk severe punishment by truth-telling, then lying becomes the strategy to avoid pain. Many black children fearing adult wrath lie. Then they struggle to cope with moral self-reproach. Seeing adults they know most intimately lie and deceive merely reinforces the notion that there is no value in being a person of integrity.

Many children create a false self early in life. In the case of black children the idea of a false self has become a norm in many families wherein folk believe that survival depends on wearing a mask, never letting anyone know how you feel or who you really are. By the time these children reach adulthood they may have no sense of who they really are. Wearing a mask requires that one learn to disassociate. Trying on different ideas, using dissimulation to con others, is one of the ways individuals choose a course of behavior that can lead to mental illness. The impostor syndrome has become more pronounced among African Americans. Individuals lie daily about where they have attended school, the degrees they have, to create a persona that works in whatever setting they may find themselves. One of my brilliant students shared with me that she was dining with a group of white folks and another black person present engaged her in a rigorous discussion about the nature of anthropological research. When he questioned her about the information she put forth, she blithely told him she was an anthropologist. Her intense desire to best him in the argument made her feel that it was fine to tell a lie. She was satisfied because she had won and wanted to minimize her lie. Yet continual acts of lying like this could easily become the behavior norm, undermining her integrity.

Our news media eagerly brings us stories about individual black people who are "impostors," such as the black female journalist who wrote a series of articles about a black boy who did not exist. When it was discovered that she had created a false story, colleagues checked out her background and found that she had lied about her educational training. Yet no articles about her case looked at the issue of self-esteem.

Years ago I recommended a black woman student, who was about to complete a master's degree, for a teaching job. When she came to the college for her interview she told them she had completed her work. This information was shared with me by the members of the all-white hiring committee. However, I knew that she had not written her thesis. They offered her the job. Hearing this, I felt a moral dilemma. I did not want to "expose" her as a liar to the committee, but I did not want to be included in a scam either. I spoke with the dean and told him that I was excited that they wanted her and felt it was in the best interests of her progress and our students to insist that her thesis be completed. I felt strongly that if she were hired with everyone knowing about her dishonesty it would set a bad example for students. I was particularly concerned that students would get the false impression that it

all parts of our lives. This is why it is important to consistently live our values.

When Nathaniel Branden first began to write about self-esteem, he acknowledged that this nation was moving into dangerous habits of being through the condoning of corruption in everyday life. Insightfully, he writes: "The challenge for people, and it is not an easy one, is to maintain high personal standards while feeling that one is living in a moral sewer. Grounds for such a feeling are to be found in the behavior of our public figures, the horror of world events, and in our so-called art and entertainment, so much of which celebrates depravity, cruelty, and mindless violence. All contribute to making the practice of personal integrity a lonely and heroic undertaking." Everyone struggles with issues of personal integrity in a nation where the belief that anyone can be bought if the price is right prevails. African Americans, economically disenfranchised for so long, have been and are particularly vulnerable when offered unprecedented economic gain for participation in activities that demand devaluation of self and others.

Even though we all live in a culture that would have everyone in this nation believe that anything we do that gives us money, especially wealth, is somehow exempt from moral scrutiny, we can and must resist such thinking if we want to have psychological well-being. Until we challenge wholeheartedly this thinking, many African Americans will collectively be the victims of crippling low self-esteem. To live with integrity we must dare to choose on behalf of our moral good, creating the necessary culture of accountability.

5

Refusing to Be a Victim

No black person in the United States can have any measure of self-esteem if he or she has not cultivated the capacity to be a critical thinker, to live consciously. Used politically in relationship to governments, the term *decolonize* means to allow to become self-governing or independent. In a personal sense decolonizing the mind means letting go of patterns of thought and behavior that prevent us from being self-determining. Since our society is structured around the principles of imperialist white supremacist, capitalist patriarchy, it is structured in such a way to impede the construction of emotional well-being for the vast majority of citizens. However, the democratic policies of our nation make it possible for everyone to resist the socialization of the thoughts, values, and actions that perpetuate imperialist white supremacist, capitalist patriarchy if they are able to learn critical thinking.

Born into a culture of domination wherein everyone is socialized to varying degrees to hate and fear "blackness," black people can create positive self-esteem only by resisting this way of thinking. This resistance takes the form of critical consciousness. In *Six Pillars of Self-Esteem* Nathaniel Branden identifies consciousness as "the basic tool of survival—the ability to be aware of the environment in some form, at some level, and to guide action accordingly." Consciousness is the ability to be aware, to have, as Branden states, "the option of exercising our powers or of subverting our means of survival and well-being." Critical consciousness is a process by which we reflect from that interrogative standpoint on our awareness of reality. For example, most black people are conscious that we live in a racist and white supremacist society. This is a basic state of awareness almost all black people hold. Critical consciousness is at work when we are able to utilize our knowledge of this reality in ways that circumvent racist exploitation and oppression.

Plainly put, parents of black children, who are aware that they live in a racist society that negatively stereotypes their children, may act in a critically conscious way by turning off the television set because it is the primary propaganda machine of white supremacist thought, or providing their children with positive images that counter the representations imposed by the dominant culture of whiteness. For many years in our nation the everyday survival of black people demanded that they develop basic skills of critical thinking. During the long period of racial apartheid black folk had to be critically vigilant to be always aware of how the system that was exploiting and oppressing them worked and as aware of what needed to be done to intervene in this system. Choosing to be unconscious or unaware easily led to severe punishment or death.

In many ways like abused children in a family system, African-American slaves became hypervigilant, obsessively monitoring the movements and behavior of their masters and mistresses so as to exercise whatever control they could within a structure that was out of control. As long as brutal racial apartheid existed and white people could dominate black people at will, critical vigilance was constantly needed to ensure black survival. Like many situations where something constructive emerges from a negative circumstance, the critical consciousness African Americans developed to resist racist exploitation and oppression has been a catalyst stimulating the overall urge to live a conscious life.

Gaining civil rights and economic prosperity led many black Americans to relax both their critical vigilance in relation to whiteness as well as their awareness of the importance of living consciously. Explaining the nature of living consciously, Nathaniel Branden writes: "Living consciously implies respect for the facts of reality. This means the facts of our inner world (needs, wants, emotions) as well as of the outer world. . . . Living consciously is living responsibly toward reality. We do not necessarily have to like what we see, but we recognize that that which is, is, and that which is not, is not. Wishes or fears or denial do not alter facts. If I desire a new outfit but need the money for rent, my desire does not transform reality and make the purchase rational." Living consciously was and continues to be an oppositional practice for black people.

Many African Americans entered the post–civil rights era weary of being critically conscious. They fantasized that equal rights in a democratic nation would mean that they would no longer have to bear the burden of hypervigilance or sustained critical consciousness. Like other Americans, especially white folks, they made freedom synonymous with not needing to be critically aware. They imagined that they could be free like everyone else, like white Americans. In their minds the ultimate freedom, the freedom they felt white folks had, was the freedom to remain aware, to have the privilege of walking through life in a unconscious dream state. And even though the racist assaults on black people continued in everyday life, many black people not only abandoned their critical vigilance, they stopped exercising critical consciousness. Trying to live consciously came to be seen as an obstacle to getting ahead.

When freedom came and black folks were compelled by the continued circumstances of domination to recognize that civil rights had not brought an end to racism and white supremacy, many folks did not want to return to the rigorous struggle that had previously characterized black experience. The perseverance in the face of difficulties that had been an ancestral legacy was abandoned by many black folks who began to see themselves as always and only victims.

By taking on the status of victimhood in a manner that denied all personal agency, all ability to effectively change and intervene in one's circumstance, many black folks surrendered all their power to be self-determining. Everything that happened could be blamed on racism, the system, the man. This embracing of victimization was a response in part to the nation's willingness to extend a helping hand to those black folks who did not appear to be self-determining, militant, or decolonized. All too frequently lots of black folk found that if they played the role of victim, assuming an almost minstrel-like persona, they were far more likely to receive attention and handouts than if they demanded justice, accountability, reparations.

Ironically, in the post–civil rights era racist white folk, especially those in power, imposed the identity of "victim" onto black folks then only a decade later accused black folks of whining about victimization. A resurgence of white supremacist thought and practice in the eighties and nineties coincided with the perpetuation on a national level of the misguided notion that racism had ended. Embedded in the assumption that racism was over was the notion that any black person who challenged white supremacy was either mad or whining, wanting something for nothing. All over the nation black folks faced racist backlash. And if the censoring and distortion of African-American experience coming from white supremacist channels was not strong enough to invalidate or silence black protest, then the system called on a new breed of enforcers, black folk who had internalized white supremacist thought. They could be strategically used to keep other black people in their place. In the last decade alone more books than ever before in our nation's history were published by black writers telling the American public that racism was over, that any black folk who claimed to be victimized by racism should be viewed with suspicion, that more than likely they were dishonest con artists out to get something for nothing.

John McWhorter's *Losing the Race: Self-Sabotage in Black America* is one of the most clever examples of this new writing. McWhorter tells readers any number of anecdotal stories where he interprets an individual black person's story, suggesting that he or she is a liar. Here is an example of his vituperative response to the claim that black folks are subjected to racist assault at predominantly white college campuses: "I have spent over half of my life as a black person on white campuses since the early 1980's, and the implication that white guys yelling 'nigger' out of passing cars or that anything of the sort is just a typical occurrence for the black undergraduate, or even that something like this happens to that undergraduate even once in a typical year, is nonsense, pure and simple." While I might agree with the suggestion that black students might exaggerate the number of racist encounters that they experience, clearly by his own aggressive discounting McWhorter goes to the other extreme, and his assertion appears to be as grandiose and false as the claims he critiques.

The role self-esteem plays as a force determing the fate of individual black folks is not discussed at any length in McWhorter's work. Had it been considered a factor in many of the incidents McWhorter offers to show how black folks embrace what he mockingly calls "victimology," a different interpretation of why so many black folks self-sabotage would emerge. The neoconservative public he addresses his work to, a public whose thinking about race continues to be informed by the values and dictates of white supremacist logic, are not interested in the way issues of self-esteem lead individual black folks to be self-sabotaging.

While I am in agreement with any social critic who holds the opinion that way too many black folks have embraced the idea that they are victims with no agency, it is clear that the refusal to assume responsibility for self has reached epidemic proportions in the society as whole. Black people who see themselves as always and only victims have embraced a way of thinking about their fate that dooms them. Yet their nihilism is not merely self-chosen, it is a reflection of the nihilism expressed in mass media. McWhorter states: "Victimology seduces young black people just like the crack trade seduces inner-city blacks, virtually irresistible in its offer of an easy road to self-esteem and some cheap thrills on the way." Black folks who see themselves as victims are sorely lacking in self-esteem, which leads them to fall prey to thinking that they lack any meaningful agency. Very few black people gain significant rewards by pretending to be victims. However, large numbers of black folks would rather be seen as victims than not seen at all.

One of the most powerful methods of psychological terrorism used by white supremacists (whether white or nonwhite) was and continues to be rendering black folks invisible.

Psychoanalytically speaking, we become subjects through a process of acknowledgment. Black folks who believed that equality meant that their full humanity would be acknowledged by whites were shattered when they were faced with painful disacknowledgment. For example many black students who enter predominantly white educational structures believing themselves the equals of their white peers, when repeatedly treated, however benevolently, as second class, not only begin to doubt their equality, many begin to perform on the level of racist white expectations. A confirmation bias is then put in place. White teachers expecting black students to perform less well than their white counterparts convey these beliefs in both conscious and unconscious behaviors in the classrooms and usually get the less than equal results they expected in the first place.

While conservative critics such as McWhorter can mock individual black folks who claim to be the victims of continual racist assault, however relative, in predominantly white settings, by doing this they discount the reality that these accounts of racist shaming may be exaggerated precisely because the longing and need for white approval is so intense. If an individual black person is longing for someone white to embrace them wholeheartedly and that white person greets them lukewarmly or with fear and mild disinterest, then the individual black person in question might easily interpret this response as an assault. The nature of this assault may be exaggerated in direct proportion to the underlying pain or internalized self-hatred it triggers. Any critic of self-sabotage in black American life who refuses to acknowledge the role self-esteem plays in how we experience and interpret the encounters we have with the white world will create theories that will be tragically flawed.

Though terribly inadequate and flawed, much of the work that looks at the failures of black Americans and claims to offer explanations, especially work that deflects attention away from the persistence of everyday racism, is accepted without question. And in the case of work like McWhorter's, it is wholeheartedly endorsed by white supremacist thinkers of any color precisely because it downplays the reality of racism and racial terrorism, denying not only the extent to which black folks are targeted but nonblack participation in these acts.

When black folks address the issue of everyday racism, naming how it impinges on our day-to-day well-being only to be accused of exaggerating, individuals whose self-esteem is fragile come to fear naming what hurts. And yet this repression is itself dangerous, because it promotes psychological implosion. Time and time again black folks talk about feeling "crazy" when they name racism and its impact only to have their stories discounted. This discounting is a form of psychological terrorism that has been used to silence antiracist protest. And it supports racist backlash by encouraging masses of white folks, and other nonblack groups, to see black folks as insane when they discuss victimization.

Living consciously, black folks today must search for ways to talk about the impact of racism on our lives that do not lead to any perpetuation of the notion that we are always and only victims. Unenlightened mass media has served as a covert propaganda machine for white supremacist thought, skillfully manipulating representations to convey to black folks and everyone else the notion, however false, that black life is horrible, that black people are the enemy, dangerous to themselves and others. The misguided message that black folks are victimizing themselves and calling it racism has become such a popular theme in our nation's mass media that there is little or no effort to challenge it.

Significantly, the black folks who see themselves as always and only victims are as deluded as those black folks who insist that black people are not victimized by ongoing racist assault on all fronts. They represent the two sides of the abused psyche, the grandiose and the unworthy. The reality falls in between these two extremes. While racist assaults happen daily in our lives, they are not necessarily victimizing, or even worthy of note. Concurrently, extreme incidents of racist victimization happen and the wounded are left unattended and justice does not prevail. Positive self-esteem requires us to be capable of responding to reality as it is, and that means acknowledging the reality of racism and working on behalf of antiracist justice. If those black folks among us who are fortunate in that they rarely encounter racism or are rarely, if ever, the victims of unjust racist attack refuse to acknowledge that they are lucky and privileged, that they are unique, then they will not be able or willing to join the struggle to end racism. They cannot respond responsibly to the crisis facing black folks in this nation.

Taking responsibility for our lives as black folks requires us to eschew assuming the role of victim even as we dare to courageously stand against racist domination. Concurrently, individual black folks who see themselves as victims should not be rebuked or scorned, since the practice of positive self-esteem demands self-acceptance. Accepting ourselves as we are is paradoxically the first stage in the process of transformation. If an individual black person who sees himself as always and only a victim accepts this reality, he is far more likely to find the agency to question this choice and change it than someone in the same predicament who resolutely refuses to acknowledge his embrace of a victim identity. Since the organized mass-based civil rights movement for racial justice ended in this nation, black folks have been systematically taught victimhood by members of the dominant white culture who feel threatened when black people fail to behave like subordinated dependent victims.

In his important work *Taking Responsibility: Self-Reliance and the Accountable Life,* Nathaniel Branden states: "If implicitly, we teach people victimhood as their core self-identification, we are not teaching self-responsibility. We are teaching dependency and impotence. The danger is that they will feel 'Someone's got to do something!' and that if the rescuer does not come, they are doomed." It is always ironic when white folks who embrace white supremacist thinking discuss the issue of self-responsibility for African Americans. Many conservative whites who are antiwelfare, who continue to represent welfare as a "black thing" when there are many more white folks benefiting from welfare, uphold the need for self-responsibility even as they work to keep in place the systems of domination that make it difficult (note that I say difficult, not impossible) for black folks to create healthy selfhood. Since it is the socialization into white supremacist thinking, the internalization of racial self-hatred, that is the psychological groundwork which prepares many black folks to see themselves as always and only victims, it is further mental colonization to then blame the individuals who succumb to powerful forces of indoctrination, most obviously mass media, and see themselves as victims.

Branden is correct in his assumption that folks who see themselves as victims usually become "stuck in passivity" and feel doomed. The loss of agency felt by many black folks in the post–civil rights era has created a nihilistic, doom-centered ethos in black life, particularly in the lives of the poor and underclass. Black folks with class privilege who may not despair about their own circumstances are often among that group of negative thinkers who not only see the poor and underclass as doomed, but who actively work to see their prophecies of doom fulfilled.

To refuse to be victims all black people must willingly engage in a politics of self-reliance that upholds taking responsibility. As an expression of positive self-esteem we have to promote the value of living consciously in a society where everyone is encouraged to remain unconscious. All around in the world, in the most dreadful situations of war and prolonged holocaust, heroic individuals have relied on their capacity to assume a degree of responsibility, however relative, over their lives to ensure their survival. African-American history documents the incredible struggles and triumphs of black people working to maintain positive thinking and action in the face of oppression and exploitation. This legacy was once the basis of African-American self-reliance and self-determination.

This spirit of living consciously and of taking responsibility was upheld by religious practice. When Christian ethics, reinforced by an active church experience, were the norm for all African Americans, religious teachings helped instill a culture of accountability. During the seventies, when atheism and fundamental shifts in this nation's moral and ethical values began to be a norm, black communities suffered. As established churches began to become more corrupt, more concerned with money-making and flashy lifestyles, the power of Christian-based self-determination was diminished. The dismantling of predominantly black educational institutions where the teaching of self-love and positive self-esteem was organically a part of the curriculum was strategically useful for the covert maintenance of racial inequality. All-black schools were among the places where individual black people learned self-reliance.

Integrated into a system that deemphasized the importance of free will while focusing on social determinism, many black people felt psychologically destabilized. Clearly, the nineteenth and early twentieth centuries' focus on racial uplift highlighted the necessity of self-esteem in ways that were soon forgotten in the post–civil rights period. During the militant years of black power astute black critical thinkers created a small body of literature focusing on self-determination. Poet and educator Haki Madhubuti (then named Don L. Lee) published his insightful treatise *From Plan to Planet: Life Studies: The Need for Afrikan Minds and Institutions* in the early seventies. He called on all African Americans to decolonize their minds and live consciously. Calling for personal and organizational development in the context of a black nationalist perspective, he urged black folks to become critical thinkers, to establish accountability and credibility, stating that it was important for us "to create an atmosphere of security and love and exemplify that in everything that you do." Yet as black power militancy lost momentum because of racial integration that offered economic reward for assimilation into the dominant culture, the essential focus on self-determination was overshadowed.

Hence more than twenty years later black people must once again reconsider the issue of self-determination. Our collective failure to create a culture where positive self-esteem is the norm for all black folks requires reevaluation and revision. While small enclaves of black nationalists continue to uphold the principles of black self-determination, they have little impact on the lives of most black people who are integrationist. A theory and practice of self-reliance must emerge that addresses black folks in the complexity and diversity of our experience. Then we can create a culture of accountability where the choice to live consciously can be freely made by all.

6

Thinking Critically

Education for critical consciousness is necessary if we are to create a sustained cultural context for black folks to have healthy self-esteem. During the period of racial segregation in our nation, when the vast majority of black folks were involved in a politics of racial uplift, segregated schools were the location where black students were encouraged to embrace education as the necessary path to freedom. In our all-black schools we were taught standards of excellence in relation to both our academic studies and our construction of self and identity. The ethics and values we were taught in our schools mirrored those taught in home and church. In our schools we were taught the value and importance of self-love.

Since the very existence of segregated schools was a constant reminder of the way in which the white majority culture saw us as intellectually inferior, the all-black school of the forties and fifties was a place where the politics of racial uplift were constantly preached. We were told that we had to be smarter than our white peers (these peers we never saw). We had to be smarter than they were to embody a direct challenge to white supremacist thinking about the inferiority of the black race.

Like many African Americans who attended all-black

schools in the segregated south and were compelled to deseg-
regate in junior high or high school, I experienced firsthand
the difference between the two educational systems. While
our teachers in the all-black schools were not always as quali-
fied as the white teachers, while our materials were often not
as current and overall resources were scarce, in the all-black
environment we were not only seen as able learners, we were
expected to be high achievers. Clearly, there were students
among us who resisted learning, students who failed, but
there were many more students who excelled. In those schools
where every teacher was black, it was a given that black folks
should strive for academic excellence in every arena. In those
days it would have seemed ludicrous for anyone to suggest
that striving to educate ourselves was a way to turn our backs
on blackness.

There were many folks in all-black schools who used white
bourgeois culture as their standard to structure manners and
etiquette, thus creating a culture of assimilation where
"whiteness" was deemed better even though no whites were
around. And there were also progressive black folks who had
decolonized their minds, who knew firsthand the value of
education for critical consciousness, who were interested in
laying the groundwork for black children to build healthy
self-esteem. Whether one wanted to speak French, play the
violin, recite Shakespeare daily, or focus on quantum physics,
none of these choices meant that one was trying not to be
black. By failing to look at the way in which the segregated
school where teachers and students were black was a terrain of
resistance when the issue was self-esteem, the civil rights
activists who wanted to integrate schools so that black children would have equal access to quality education unwittingly set the stage for the colonization of young black minds

by a poisonous pedagogy embedded in education at the hands of white colonizers.

Schools were integrated late in the southern world of my upbringing. My sense of self and black identity had been firmly formed in the world of all-black schools where teachers were dedicated both to academic excellence and to laying the groundwork for healthy self-esteem. When the state demanded school desegregation, black parents in our communities did meet to discuss whether integrated schools would be the best setting for black children to learn. Even when they voiced grave doubts, there was the assumption that the first groups of black children to enter these white schools in areas where overt white supremacy was the norm were warriors for racial justice. We were prepared to sacrifice comfort for the cause of equality.

Like so many Americans in the late fifties and early sixties, black folks were convinced that racism was due to ignorance, that if folks knew better they would act better. Our parents never warned us about white teachers being racist. Most of our teachers were covertly racist. Like my beloved high school drama teacher, a young white woman, more liberal than conservative, but somewhere in between the two, who nurtured my talent even as she also shared with me her conviction that I would not find a black husband because I was too smart. Racism and sexism informed her perceptions of black masculinity; she had no experience with black males. She felt she was preparing me for the real world, so I would understand the price I would pay for choosing to be an educated, independent woman. When I encountered her in my adult years and we spoke of this time, she expressed regret for any biases she had expressed, calling attention to her own youthfulness at the time and all that she had not unlearned about racism.

While her perspective on black life interested me, it never carried the weight of my family values, of my experience in an all-black community where smart black women mated and married black men.

Naturally, black parents raised in brutal racial apartheid in the south were initially more conscientious when the schools were desegregated and their children were about to be educated by the very same white folks who had proclaimed the need for segregation because of black inferiority. They were mindful of the ways we were taught. When I came home in the late sixties and told my parents that my white teachers were so dumb that they told us black people had not written books, we saw this as just another gesture of white arrogance. It would not have occurred to us to allow ourselves to be the victims of this racist ignorance. Given the white supremacist milieu of the times, no one assumed that white schools would provide us information about blackness.

In retrospect it is difficult to pinpoint exactly why this critical vigilance in regard to race and education diminished. Certainly a combination of factors led black folks to feel that they could cease the hypervigilance that had surrounded all interactions between white people and black people prior to full-scale desegregation. Among these factors, the strongest was the belief that black power militancy had created the sustained cultural context for black self-love. Another factor was the rise in liberal individualism. Racial integration made it possible for black folks to see more clearly that all white people did not think alike. When large numbers of individual black students were welcomed into predominantly white colleges, when efforts were made to integrate and diversify public and private schools, many black parents felt that the racial equality so long sought after and struggled for had finally arrived. The widespread institutionalization of black studies brought more black teachers into the picture in higher education.

Even though militant black power activists consistently critiqued mainstream educational institutions, the reality was simply that a huge majority of black folks were more conservative than radical. They were not listening to the militant voices that argued it was cultural genocide to let white folks teach black children. In 1972 Don L. Lee declared: "To intrust the minds of our young to Europeans is equivalent to blowing their brains out ourselves, for all we will receive in return are brothers and sisters who are confused about their identity, purpose, and direction, and in effect have been tortured to a slow death." Despite the positive impact of black power efforts to increase civil rights for all black people, most black folks did not really endorse the pan-Africanism that formed the core of black nationalist thinking. When writers such as Amiri Baraka called attention to the fact that unenlightened white folks would work to colonize the minds of black children, very few black parents took these warnings seriously.

Countering the notion of the natural superiority of whites, Baraka stated that whites excelled because of "their ability to physically and mentally hold everybody else back while at the same time on many levels build, invent, and create for their own interest at the expense of others." But the education for critical consciousness young black militants acquired by reading Nkrumah, Fanon, Memmi, interspersed with Mao Tsetung, Ho Chi Minh, and the radical works by men from all over the world did not reach the black masses. And when it did, everyday black folks were often more suspicious of the idealization of Africa presented by militant black radicals than they were of the racist white teachers educating their young. By the midseventies there were a number of small predominantly black schools in urban areas where black power militancy had the greatest impact on the daily lives of black folks.

Consistently working to create schools that would serve the interests of black students, Haki Madhubuti (then Don L. Lee), like his comrades in struggle, was mindful of the fact that black folks were increasingly absorbing mainstream values, defined in the vernacular as wanting to be white. Lee stated:

> If we, as a people, are so busy trying to be white, trying to love white, trying to act and live white in a world that will only accept us if we are actually white—we should be in the position that we're in. To want to be white in a world where the majority of the people are of color is a sickness. To have internalized the values and aspirations of the oppressor to such a degree again emphasizes the need of a people to educate its own, if it wishes to keep its own. To turn our children over to others is to run the risk of losing them forever.

Ironically, rather than being lost forever in a world of whiteness, many black students in predominantly white schools, taught by biased and uncaring teachers, simply dropped out. During the seventies and eighties many black students entered predominantly white colleges and universities only to leave without acquiring degrees. Usually the radical consciousness around race they acquired made it difficult to sit quietly in classrooms where most teachers covertly distorted facts and information in the interest of maintaining white supremacist thinking. When challenged, these educators usually used their power to negate these critiques, either by shaming black students in the classroom or failing them. Individual black students who imitated the thinking and actions of white peers, who assimilated, were more likely to succeed.

While progressive black schools existed on the grade school and high school levels, militant black radicals had not founded institutions of higher education. There was no radical alternative for the black college student who wanted education for critical consciousness, as black institutions of higher learning were as conservative, if not more so, than their white counterparts. Black students who decolonized their minds, who stayed in predominantly white institutions, learned to seek out the liberal and radical professors of any race to further their education. Sadly, students who had been raised with a nationalist perspective found it difficult to enter a work world where they had to know how to relate to the very white folks black power rhetoric had demonized. They had nowhere to turn. Even though some of them went to Africa and found there a welcoming climate of solidarity, they were, after all, citizens of the United States who had to, at some point, return home.

Black students seeking to educate themselves for critical consciousness in a context where they could build healthy self-esteem were really caught in a bind. If they were not pan-African in their thinking, they could not be accepted in the black nationalist circles; if they looked for sanctuary in liberal and radical white circles, they had to confront racism.

Sadly, by the early eighties it had become clear to everyone that black children were not being adequately educated in the public schools. Poor black children suffered the most neglect. Overcrowding, disciplinary problems, a dearth of visionary teachers all led to the continuation and growth of poisonous pedagogy, teaching that overtly reflected white supremacist thinking. Whether white or nonwhite, more often than not teachers in the public school system held racist assumptions about black students or found it difficult, even if they had so desired, to question the overt racism of teaching plans and materials. Like visionary black teachers in the pre–civil rights all-black school, antiracist teachers of any race found and find themselves constricted by established curriculum that sanctions and normalizes racist thinking.

Given this context, who can truly express surprise that troubled black children, echoing the biases of racist educators, begin to declare their own war on education? They not only begin to actively resist learning, they begin to terrorize those black children who want to learn. Much is made of this fact by conservative critics who see it as evidence of the natural inferiority of black children or as evidence of some innate self-sabotaging structure. However, they deny that the primary source of the problem was a racist and racially biased educational system that was never transformed so that it could welcome all students and offer education as the practice of freedom. Black students are acting in a self-destructive manner when they repudiate all education, but low self-esteem makes it easier to reject the faulty education that is offered rather than do the work, which black folks did in the past, of taking the learning that was needed for our advancement and leaving the rest.

In recent years more black folks have recognized the way in which racially biased curriculum and racist teachers (of all colors) fail black children, and yet the solution to this problem they present is usually a return to a nationalist-based education. Progressive action that could liberate and challenge the minds of black children need not be nationalist. But there is still little focus in our nation on creating learning environments that are antiracist in structure and in content, which address the specific needs of black students while remaining inclusive.

Black nationalist educators insightfully recognize more than other groups that black children cannot receive an education that will provide a foundation for healthy self-esteem in settings that are designed to uphold and maintain white supremacy. What nationalist educators often fail to recognize is that merely being taught by teachers who are black has not and will not solve the problem if the teachers have been socialized to internalize racist thinking.

Any black person who clings to the misguided notion that white people represent the embodiment of all that is evil and black people all that is good remains wedded to the very logic of Western metaphysical dualism that is the heart of binary racist thinking. Such thinking is not liberatory. Like the racist educational ideology it mirrors and imitates, it invites a closing of the mind. Hence it can never promote the critical thinking that is essential for the maintenance of healthy self-esteem. A black person with healthy self-esteem can maintain the integrity of their being whether they are in a racially segregated or integrated context.

In our nation most black people work in racially integrated settings but, like their counterparts of other races, they mostly socialize after work in segregated settings. They may justify this difference by saying that they are more comfortable hanging out with folks like themselves. However, the truth is often that they present a false self at work and need a space where they can unmask. People with healthy self-esteem do not need to create pretend identities. At its very best education should strengthen our capacity to be fully self-actualized in whatever setting we find ourselves.

Education as the practice of freedom requires a holistic approach to learning. In such a setting every interaction in the classroom matters—not just the information teachers impart. The way they engage with students matters and will determine whether or not a learning community forms. Learning rarely takes place in a hostile environment. When I was a college student taking classes from professors who taught from racist perspectives, who often used shaming and other covert forms of psychological terrorism to undermine the self-esteem of nonwhite students, I adapted by enduring and pre-severing in the face of these barriers, but I never felt I enjoyed school. Learning in an environment of anxiety and stress has caused many black folks to lose their faith in the transformative power of education. But the problem was never education but rather being taught by narrow-minded educators.

Education as the practice of freedom has never been available to any significant body of black folks. Learning how to be a conscious critical thinker places any individual in an outsider position in a culture of domination that rewards conformity. In the contemporary world black identities are diverse and complex; consequently we need a variety of educational settings to make education for critical consciousness the norm. More antiracist progressive teachers, of any race, are needed if schools and colleges are to participate in the holistic self-recovery of black folks and affirm the reality that it is possible to achieve healthy self-esteem within the existing culture of domination. Education, as it is, had been the primary tool of fascist racism, perpetuating and upholding misinformation. Without serious ongoing educational reform, education will continue to mirror the plantation culture where the slave was allowed to learn only those forms of knowledge that justified continued enslavement. If black folks want to be free, they must want to be educated. Without freedom of mind there can be no true and lasting freedom.

give us a well-rounded education, one where black history and culture are affirmed. Any examination of those periods in American history where African Americans have been engaged in organized transformation in the interest of civil rights and freedom reveals an intense focus on reading. In the wake of civil rights and black power antiracist movement black writers wrote an amazing body of nonfiction work aimed at educating other black people. The purpose of this literature was to provide a mass-based audience with the information and knowledge that would serve as the basis for critical thinking. This was a literature of resistance; its purpose was to educate and transform consciousness. From the late sixties to the end of the seventies, on public transportation all around the United States black folks of all classes could be seen reading the works of Gwendolyn Brooks, Don L. Lee (Haki Madhubuti), LeRoi Jones (Amiri Baraka), James Baldwin, Audre Lorde, Malcolm X, Alex Haley, Eldridge Cleaver, George Jackson, Sonia Sanchez, Toni Bambara, Mari Evans, and a host of other black thinkers and writers who were bringing the word to the people.

Often the messages of education for critical consciousness first came to the people through performance art, in places where music and the spoken word converged. This configuration, particularly the use of popular music to express political self-determination, enabled learning to take place that did not depend on literacy. Significantly, individual black folks, especially black males, were often compelled to read more, either to learn to read for the first time or to improve their reading skills, because they hungered for the new knowledge that led them in the direction of black liberation.

During this period black-owned and -operated publications were abundant. It was an accepted given that one could not go to the ethnocentric racist white press and expect it to publish militant dissident work. Yet corporate white publishing did recognize the value of this new reading material and made its interest known by publishing bestselling works such as *Soul on Ice, The Autobiography of Malcolm X, Black Macho and the Myth of the Superwoman.* These works were read by black folks from all classes. Prison writing, both letters and books, carried the message that it was possible for incarcerated black men to educate themselves for critical consciousness through reading. In his life stories Malcolm X shared that reading and critical thinking led to the formation of critical consciousness.

This was the period of my critical political awakening. I came to consciousness at the end of the sixties. During my first year of college I read the necessary texts required for an English major and I devoured the work of black writers and thinkers. Now and then these writers were taught in newly formed ethnic studies classes, but for the most part I found them through conversation with dissident thinkers of all races. And once again, as in my childhood when I found more black writers by going to the public library, I turned again to libraries to fill the gap. This was an amazing time, because the prevailing mood was one of resistance and transformation. Militant black power leaders were calling all black folks to take responsibility for building healthy self-esteem. Reading the right books was deemed essential for self-actualization.

Much of the work black writers published, such as Don L. Lee's *From Plan to Planet: Life Studies for Afrikan Minds and Institutions,* had long book lists at the end to guide the reader to further work. Lee's book was published by Broadside Press Institute of Positive Education; it cost $1.95. There were many similar works circulated as pamphlets. Even though many of these new black thinkers were coming from middle-class backgrounds, they were addressing their message to the black masses, and by so doing they continued a tradition of antiracist resistance, which encouraged all black folks to read and write, to develop critical consciousness.

This focus on reading, writing, and publishing was a crucial intervention because it helped lay the groundwork for a public cultural context where the development of black self-esteem could be identified as a personal and political necessity for all black people. Conversation, dialogues about the issues, were a vital part of this cultural revolution. When we read about the lives of militant black power advocates we learned that many of them were challenged by interactions with critically conscious friends and acquaintances to educate themselves. The consciousness-raising group, the political rally, the political discussion taking place at the social hour were all spaces where individuals could find support for education for critical consciousness. This was cultural revolution at its best; it promoted dialogue, debate, dialectical exchange. And in this atmosphere of independent thinking black folks were learning how to decolonize our minds and build healthy self-esteem.

The systematic murder of black leaders was a conscious political effort on the part of the imperialist white supremacist, capitalist patriarchal state to stop this cultural revolution. State-sponsored and/or supported terrorism sent the message that black folks who challenged the existing status quo risked their lives. The destruction of militant black organizations, the seduction of an assimilation-based desegregation model, all encouraged black folks to turn away from dissident thought. Racial integration was the political shift diffusing black militancy. If black folks could be perceived as having gained a measure of social equality within the existing structure, then there was no need for further protest. Integration was the location where black folks were invited to embrace the ethic of liberal individualism, to move away from the notion of communal racial uplift that had been at the core of black nationalist politics, of militant black liberation struggle. The demise of a mass-based political movement for self-determination effectively diffused, and in many cases eliminated, the cultural context for a mass-based movement for critical consciousness that pushed the primacy of education.

By the early eighties black nationalist thinking and practice was reduced to a subcultural phenomenon, seen as mainly relevant to disenfranchised classes of "inferior" black folks who were represented as lacking the skills and know-how to successfully make use of the rights and privileges awarded them by mainstream white culture. Middle- and upper-class black folks, witnessing the ravaged self-esteem of a new group of black folks raised in predominantly white settings where racist thinking and action was the norm, began to turn in the direction of lifestyle-based nationalism, i.e., trips to Africa, wearing ethnic clothing, natural hairstyles. The radical emphasis on education for critical consciousness had diminished. Oftentimes these individuals were white-identified black folks who had tried to assimilate only to find that they were not fully accepted as equals in the white world no matter how they behaved. It is the group of people Ellis Cose writes about in his book *The Rage of a Privileged Class.* Turning away from whiteness toward romantic nationalism, these groups of privileged black folks often still suffered from the crippling low self-esteem that led them to overidentify with some idealized notion of whiteness in the first place. Often their embrace of blackness was just as idealized, their bond with

"Africa" a fantasy bond. In both cases the idealization masks deep insecurities and feelings of lack providing pseudo self-esteem.

A distinction must be made between the healthy self-esteem that necessarily ensures that an individual will learn about their past, their ethnic heritage, and the pseudo self-esteem that is created by utopian fantasies of the past. Healthy self-esteem allows us to accept and love ourselves just the way we are (and that includes race), while recognizing at the same time that we are always more than identities we cannot change (sex, race, etc.). Clearly, it has been detrimental to the self-esteem of black folks to be focused on race as though that is the only aspect of identity that has meaning. No wonder then that black folks hoped that equal rights would lead to an end to racism—to not having to live in a world where race mattered too much.

As racial integration brought greater job and career opportunities for black people, especially educated black folks, the will to make money began to replace the will to be free, to decolonize one's mind, to be independent thinkers. Many black people felt that there was no need for continued militant antiracist resistance in the eighties. They felt either that the struggle was over or that white America simply was never going to realize the democratic ideal of equal rights, and that the one place where individual black folks could find satisfaction was through making and spending money. The culture of hedonistic consumerism did not place an emphasis on reading, writing, or critical thinking. As more black folks adopted middle-class values, often imitating the manners and mores of the white people they denounced as racist, they became more concerned with the trappings of success than with racial uplift. More and more privileged black folks were no longer concerned with the plight of the black poor and disenfranchised. As public school systems evolved more and more into a pseudo prison where poor black children are detained and held rather than educated, the focus on education as a path to freedom and self-actualization ended.

The embrace of bourgeois and upper-class values by all black folks who allowed their worldview to be shaped by the class politics of television meant that a high value began to be placed on conformity of thought and action. For subordinated groups of black people, the poor and underclass, the primary value was that of obedience. Rather than acting as conscious consumers, black folks have allowed their habits of thought and being to be informed by the racially unenlightened world of advertising and mass media. As independent thinking is central to the development of healthy self-esteem, the insistence on following the cultural codes of middle- and upper-class decorum disrupted efforts to create a cultural context where black folks could learn to identify self-worth with volitional choice, with independent thinking. And there was no huge body of literature focusing on decolonization, self-determination, and self-love that ensured a continued focus on the issue of self-esteem.

White corporate publishing recognized the new black consumer, but the books that were increasingly pitched to this group were more often than not popular fiction. Even so, serious fiction by black writers received more attention as well. However, the vast majority of books published and marketed in the direction of black folks often reinforced negative stereotypes. Only now because the writer was black and making money, this work was not subjected to the kinds of critique and boycotting that would have taken place at a time when race consciousness and the concern for racial uplift was strong. If the sixties and seventies were characterized by the publishing of reading material aimed at racial uplift, self-determination, and attempts to understand race and racism in this nation while working to realize democratic ideals, the eighties and nineties offered the literature of fantasy and escape. More than ever before it was apparent to the American public, especially publishers, that there was indeed a black reading public. But the books that public devoured with great intensity were popular fiction drawing on many of the negative stereotypes black folks had only a few years back argued did not define the nature of black identity or black experience.

Very little of this literature deals with the issue of self-esteem. Most of the characters in fiction that focus on blackness are portraits of self-hating individuals who are unable to live consciously. One of the most popular works of fiction, Terry McMillan's *Waiting to Exhale,* showed black professional women obsessed with finding a mate and subjecting themselves to all manner of psychological self-mutilation to get and keep a man. This focus on looking outside the self for validation and self-esteem continues to send the message that black folks cannot create an inner world that will sustain self-love. The poor self-concept of the black women in this novel and in similar works is accepted as natural and normative. Popular escapist fiction enchants adult readers without challenging them to be educated for critical consciousness. The success of this work affects the work published that seeks to capture younger readers.

Books marketed to black children are often the least progressive. Books such as *Nappy Hair* and *Daddy Is a Monster . . . Sometimes* perpetuate the idea that black folks are inherently flawed and incapable of kind and moral behavior. These representations have much in common with the racist iconography of the nineteenth century. Much of the children's literature published since the seventies with black children as the perceived audience reinforces the racist assumption that black children are really mini adults. Illustrations in books aimed at young black readers usually depict them looking like adults in children's bodies or depict them without eyes or mouths, resembling cartoon characters rather than real people. But there are no critical avenues where any body of critically conscious antiracist readers review and critique this literature to see whether or not it undermines the self-esteem of black children. And there is so little literature aimed at black teen readers that almost any material is deemed acceptable by publishers.

Writing that stimulates education for critical consciousness exists but it is rare, hard to find, and often expensive. New technologies and the world of video and computers have usurped the place of reading in the lives of many children, especially black children, and the lives of many adults. In recent years the rare book that black people across class run out to buy and read is usually antiblack or aggressively promoting dysfunction. A perfect example of this trend was the short-lived popularity of Shahrazad Ali's *The Black Man's Guide to Understanding the Black Woman*. In this book Ali shared that black women were nasty and smelled bad, that black men needed to use physical violence to keep females in check. A mixture of fundamentalist religious teachings about the inherent evils of the female and racist, sexist stereotypes in blackface, this book was embraced by black folks of all classes. Ali was on national television. Now only a few years later no one even mentions her work. Yet in black communities and with the assistance of racist, sexist media helping her reach a national audience, she worked hard to publicly shame black females, especially the dysfunctional poor and disenfranchised groups. Hopefully, we will soon see a day when masses of black people will rush out to buy books that offer us life-based survival strategies rooted in self-love and a collective love of blackness that need never be exclusionary, since our love of race cannot be taken away, nor is it diminished when we openly seek community and contact with folks who are not like outselves.

If we black people want a body of literature that reinforces healthy self-esteem, then we and our allies in struggle must not only write this work, we must struggle to find publishers. These days such work can rarely compete with trashy popular fiction or conservative antiblack polemics because it is not reviewed in the white press or overall in mass media in ways that let the public know it exists. Since we no longer have a mass-based antiracist political movement, there are no public rallies or consciousness-raising groups where this literature can be talked about and shared. Positively, there are book clubs that are working to restimulate progressive discussion. And the public library still exists, despite efforts on the part of fiscal conservatives to close its doors, as a place where individuals of all classes can gain access to writing that will raise their consciousness.

If we are to see a change in the collective self-esteem of black people, reading and writing will need to be once again a central focus of racial uplift. Increasingly, black folks are counted among the huge numbers of citizens of this society who cannot read or write. Reports released in recent years indicate that black males are at a higher risk for illiteracy than any group of native-born English speakers. When computers are deemed by advertising to be the only way to gain knowledge, then consumers who cannot afford them may just drop out. Concurrently, as books become more expensive, as unenlightened publishers continue to publish work by and about black people that merely reinforces the status quo, we will need to depend both on those bookstores that allow people to read without purchasing and on libraries to offer access to the forms of knowledge that will strengthen our self-esteem.

Certainly, in my life the issue of self-esteem was first raised in all-black schools as teachers sought to counter the received negative information about blackness and black identity coming from white supremacist culture, then raised again by militant antiracist black power protest. Indeed, no information received in school enhanced my learning to know more about the issue of self-esteem than the works of Nathaniel Branden and others that I discovered browsing in bookstores. Every day there is an individual black person unlearning racist socialization and actively building healthy self-esteem because they simply dared to look for the information that could help the trouble that they knew was ailing them. I have never encountered any person with crippling or low self-esteem who was unaware of the issue. They could name the problem but were not sure where to find the solution. When our bookshelves contain a body of work that examines from various standpoints the issue of black people and self-esteem, we will be letting the world know that no matter the forces of domination and oppression, we are accountable for our fate. With healthy self-esteem as our foundation, we will overcome.

8

Spiritual Redemption

Religion has played a crucial role in the historical development of self-esteem among African Americans. It served as a vital source of empowerment for both the small number of free Africans who came to these shores as immigrants or explorers and the large body of enslaved Africans. Fusing Christian traditions with the diverse spiritual traditions from Africa, black folks created ways to worship that were celebrating and life-sustaining. Significantly, enslaved Africans, like their free counterparts, did not uncritically embrace Christianity. They interpreted scriptures and chose texts that reinforced their humanity, their quest for liberation.

Using the Bible as a source for self-esteem, black folks were able to counter the white supremacist insistence that they were less than human. The recognition of their essential humanity enabled displaced Africans to recover the will that enslavement had endeavored to break. From the testimony of slave narratives it is evident that enslaved black folk often experienced intense despair engendered by overwhelming feelings of powerlessness. Since the intent of colonization and slavery was to strip the slave of all agency, religious experience that enabled black people to identify with enduring the suffering of bondage while maintaining one's hope was life-sustaining.

From their reading of the Bible enslaved black folks were able to envision a religion grounded in the belief that obedience to the will of God was the only necessary requirement to be chosen, to be lifted out of slavery into freedom. It was their own experience of living in hope that enabled oppressed black people to see the possibility of an end to their plight. In *The Outrageous Pursuit of Hope* Mary Grey explains via her reading of the biblical Book of Isaiah the way in which Christianity is a theology of hope. Insightfully, she contends, "This is because Isaiah . . . lived in times of imminent disaster and the threat of the destruction of the city and Temple of Jerusalem; but then, after the destruction, when the worst had actually happened, and the children of Israel were forced to live in captivity in Babylon, it was the prophetic task to keep hope alive in the shadow of, the context of, oppression." Through their religious and spirtual experience enslaved Africans not only kept hope alive, they developed a liberation theology, designed to serve as a constant reminder of their right to freedom, to citizenship, to divine love. Grey states, "The wisdom of prophetic community is both radical and subversive, as we saw in the way Isaiah kept hope alive in the Babylonian captivity." To keep hope alive, enslaved Africans created a spirituality of resistance.

To ensure their survival, they could not be content with a conservative interpretation of Christian scripture. They had to evoke what contemporary theologian Matthew Fox calls the "cosmic Christ." Sharing the insight that we are in need of "a radical religious awakening worthy of being called a spiritual renaissance," one that bring together "psyche (mysticism) and society (justice and prophecy)," he aptly describes the transformation of religious experience as interpreted by enslaved African Americans. Identifying with a god of justice, who not only chooses the poor and oppressed but especially loves them, enabled exploited and oppressed African Americans to create a basis for self-acceptance. By surrendering to their situation through recognition of the reality that as long as they were enslaved they had to restore their souls through hope, they could then strategize a spirituality of resistance that would lead to freedom.

In the world beyond slavery the radical religion of the slave began to change. As the black church became in time an organized corporate institution the religion of African Americans shifted from the liberation theology that had been so necessary for survival and settled in a conservative faith, one that relied on more fundamentalist interpretations of the Bible. This may have been a consequence of the black preacher being educated at institutions that were not only conservative but similar in kind to white institutions. It was this conservative, conformist thrust in contemporary African-American religious experience that led Martin Luther King, Jr., to give a sermon titled "Transformed Noncomformist" where he quoted from the biblical Book of Romans, scripture daring us to "be not conformed to this world: but be ye transformed by the renewing of your mind." King reminded his audience of the radically subversive nature of true Christian faith.

He warned that this new conservatism of the black church, and all Christian churches, would be dangerous for freedom. Courageously, King declared:

> Nowhere is the tragic tendency to conform more evident than in church, an institution which has often served to crystallize, conserve, and even bless the patterns of majority opinion. The erstwhile sanction by the church of slavery, racial segregation, war, and economic exploitation is testimony

to the fact that the church has hearkened more to the authority of the world than to the authority of God. Called to be the moral guardian of the community, the church at times has preserved that which is immoral and unethical.

He was especially critical of preachers who he saw as having "been tempted by the enticing cult of conformity" and "seduced by the success symbols of the world." King declared: "We preach comforting sermons and avoid saying anything from our pulpit which might disturb the respectable views of the comfortable members of our congregations." As black preachers conformed to the status quo, the Christianity they offered was not one of radical love and acceptance but more one of discipline and punishment.

Black people who embraced a more fundamentalist Christian doctrine, with its binary focus on good and evil, dark and light, chosen and unchosen, could no longer look to religion to provide a healthy basis for self-esteem. By investing in a belief system that not only deemed some folks worthy and others unworthy, but suggests it is natural for the strong to rule over the weak, that those who do not obey authority should be punished, black folk were essentially internalizing the Western metaphysical dualism that was already used to affirm and uphold domination. And even when black people did not absorb all this thinking, it created confusion and contradictions that were and are emotionally stressful. That stress has been apparent in the arena of healthy self-esteem about the body and sexuality.

The rigid body-hating doctrines of the scriptures perpetuated the notion that the body was inherently unclean, evil, corrupt, that sexuality was bad. Instead of offering black folks ways of thinking about the body that countered racist stereo-types these conservative interpretations of scripture rein-forced and promoted internalized racism. Often the color caste system that privileged light-skinned black folks over darker-skinned folks was at its worst within the established, respectable church. Prophetically, King saw that a spirituality of resistance was being replaced by an opportunistic spiritual-ity of conformity.

As young black people continued to engage antiracist struggle, they often dropped out of the church. They did not just leave behind the religion of their ancestors, they began to leave behind the belief that attending to the needs of the spirit, that spiritual life, was important for self-actualization, fulfillment, and healthy self-esteem. In *Ethics for the New Millennium* his holiness the Dalai Lama makes a useful dis-tinction between religion and spirituality, asserting:

> Religion I take to be concerned with faith in the claims to salvation of one faith tradition or another, an aspect of which is acceptance of some form of metaphysical or supernatural reality, including perhaps an idea of heaven or nirvana. Connected with this are religious teachings or dogma, ritual, prayer, and so on. Spirituality I take to be concerned with those qualities of the human spirit—such as love and compassion, patience, tol-erance, forgiveness, contentment, a sense of respon-sibility, a sense of harmony—which bring happiness to both self and others.

When contemporary black people abandon the positive ancestral legacy wherein the cultivation of spiritual practice was a necessary component of self-development, they were and are deprived of a primary foundation for the construction of healthy self-esteem.

The movement away from spiritual practice has had profound negative consequences for young black people. It has deprived them of an ethical foundation on which to make constructive moral judgments. Since the movement away from the organized black church as well as other forms of spiritual practice coincided with an overall move in the nation toward narcissistic individualism, young black folks who were tired of an ethic of communalism that had emphasized racial uplift and the community found support for solely focusing on satisfying the desires of the self. Encouraged by the cult of hedonistic consumerism as well as by the overall cultural disavowal of a belief in higher powers, many black folks could and did embrace the culture of narcissism. This choice brought them closer to unenlightened white people and other groups who were also deeply invested in liberal individualism.

Without a deeply religious or spiritual practice emphasizing the kind of values that strengthen self-esteem, responsibility, and accountability, many young black people feel morally adrift. They fall into stylish nihilism and are cynical about issues like justice and democracy. Their worldview is countered by those who cling to an old-style Christianity of the "God will take care of you" kind that diffuses the will to protest. This was the Christianity that Martin Luther King, Jr., warned against. And indeed it was the hypocrisy of the church in general, and the black church in particular, that has led so many folks away from its doors. The spirituality of resistance created and sustained by oppressed and exploited black folks was especially concerned about the poor.

Indeed, religion was the one place in our society prior to the seventies where the poor could find affirmation of their right to exist, of their humanity. Writing about my childhood experience in the church and the ideas toward the poor I learned there in *Where We Stand: Class Matters,* I state: "Again and again we were told in church that once we crossed the threshold of this holy place sanctified by divine spirit we were all one. . . . Indeed, showing solidarity with the poor was essential spiritual work, a way to learn the true meaning of community and enact the sharing of resources that would necessarily dismantle hierarchy and difference." In those days solidarity with the poor was aimed at removing the stigma of shame.

In today's world, poverty is seen as solely a mark of shame, a sign that one is not worthy or chosen. The culture of narcissism has no use for the poor. The church, once a place where the poor could find refuge and a sense of identity that could bolster wounded self-esteem, like many other institutions in our nation has all but forsaken the poor. And even those institutions that support giving material assistance to those in need deny their humanity by refusing to recognize needs of the spirit. The assumption that the poor are more in need of material help than of the resources to build healthy self-esteem is false. For without healthy self-esteem very few poor people are able to use their resources in ways that sustain their overall well-being.

When the church ceased to be an institution that promoted the self-esteem of the poor, many needy black people were left with no public support for their wounded self-esteem. Feeling shamed or rejected by the established church, poor black people can rarely find an alternative place to worship where the needs of their spirit will be affirmed. Not all established churches are corrupt, yet the more progressive the church in message and deed the least likely that poor folks will find their way to worship services there. Progressive churches are rarely located in poor communities. Faced with a religion that denies their humanity, that shames and punishes, folks turn away from godliness and cease recognizing the value of spiritual life.

In the early seventies psychiatrists William Grier and Price Cobbs published a book called *The Jesus Bag,* in which they argued that the morality black folks had shaped in liberation quest was unique and special, one that would help heal the nation as a whole. They praised the movement away from the conservative Christianity that had been used to justify racial exploitation and oppression:

> Religion made most blacks patient, but this patience wore thin under the grossness of their mistreatment. For most of our history in America, the churches counseled reliance on the law and on the good intention of whites and only recently have many churches supported organized protest. At last, blacks have psychologically untangled themselves from whites religiously and found a flowering of racial pride and a growth of black identity.

They argued that black folks had developed a "healing black morality, psychologically profound and true." Clearly, Grier and Cobbs imagined that the shift in the direction of healthy self-affirmation would be sustained.

Boldly they declared, "Religion lost its hold on some of us and the rage binding conscience was no longer effective. In a fury, we burst into the streets. We had survived the oppression and we now have survived the riots. Where we were once ashamed of the scars we now see them as badges of honor. We looked into ourselves and, even more, looked deep into white America. Our flaws, which we were taught to hide in shame, were in the flaws of this nation. The hatred we had of ourselves was minor placed alongside whites' folks hatred of us. Where once we saw ourselves as deformed and debased, we now see how much more deformed and debased is the white bigotry which has so hurt us. Black people who all that time had tried futilely to turn themselves inside out have now opened the festering wound of America and see that it is America which has most need of healing." The "black morality" Grier and Cobbs believed would remain strong in black life was eroded by despair over the violent backlash against antiracist struggle, assimilation-oriented integration that rewarded black people for supporting the status quo, and the overall embrace of consumer-based capitalism.

Indeed, the morality Grier and Cobbs perceived as being black morality mirrors the Dalai Lama's description of positive ethical conduct. He links ethical acts, which lead us to refrain from causing harm to others, and spiritual acts, which can be described in terms of "love, compassion, patience, forgiveness, humility, tolerance," through which we show our concern for the well-being of others. The Dalai Lama's insistence that we are in need of a spiritual revolution echoes the visionary call Grier and Cobbs made in their book when they declared: "We suggest rather that America turn in the direction of a new ethic." Mistakenly, Grier and Cobbs believed it was possible for black folks to flourish without attending to the needs of spiritual life, without creating religious experience that would sustain untested visions of self-development, self-actualization, and self-esteem.

Creating a cultural context for healthy black self-esteem

means that we must restore the religious locations where a spirituality that embraces lost souls can flourish. Just as the liberation theology of the past offered to African Americans a vision of a counterculture where justice could prevail, where excess and decadence were questioned, contemporary African Americans are in need of a spirituality that calls for renewal and restoration of the soul, a religion that truly celebrates coming together, reunion. When we talk about self-esteem, that reunion can take the form of returning to an emphasis on inherent divine glory that can counter the white supremacist thinking that constantly tells black folks we are unworthy.

Young black folk have asked me where can we go to find the foundations of self-love if all about us we are daily bombarded with the messages that say we are the embodiment of all that is negative. As one young woman put it, "We come out of the womb into this space where somebody right there on the spot is judging us and deciding what our fate will be on the basis of the color of our skin." She was not referring to white people but to black parents who at the child's birth are eager to see skin color and hair texture to determine the value. I shared with this young woman that this is why we need origin stories that start not with this world but with the mysterious world of the divine. King stated in his sermon on noncomformity that "every true Christian is a citizen of two worlds, the world of time and the world of eternity," that we are "paradoxically of the world and yet not of the world." The prophetic imagination offers a revisioning of origin where we can imagine ourselves outside the boundaries set by humans in a mystical universe, like the one Matthew Fox evokes wherein all souls are loved, where there is no valuation based on skin color or status. This is the cosmic Christ the enslaved Africans chose.

Even though I have focused in this chapter on Christianity, much of what has been stated about this religious faith can also be said of Islam and the other faiths black people choose to follow. More than ever before in our nation there are New Age alternatives to religion that seek to impede genuine spiritual growth. As part of our collective self-recovery African Americans must once again courageously interrogate religious and spiritual practice that stands in the way of healthy self-esteem while simultaneously seeking out those forms of religious worship and spiritual practice that affirm the integrity of our being.

9

Searching at the Source

There is no monolithic black family in the United States. And yet were we to bring together the huge body of sociological work examining the experiences of black people, we would find that black families are continually talked about as though they are all alike. No matter how many two-parent black families abound, more than ever before in our nation's history when the image of the black family is depicted it is almost always as a single-parent family. Recently, I worked with the publishers of one of my children's books on the illustration for the cover. The book was about a two-parent family and the love they give their daughter. However, the cover image that they had chosen was of a mother hugging her daughter. When I inquired about the image, suggesting that it did not convey what this book was about, the group of liberal young white people who had made this decision could not give cogent reasons for their cover choice. They expressed fondness for the image.

As a cultural critic I write endlessly about the ways blackness is represented and the power representations have to shape our sense of our self. And to me this image, though beautiful, conveyed a different message from the book. Luckily, I was in the presence of a group of people who were willing to listen to my concerns. I suggested that it is important to have positive images of single parents but it is just as important for us to have positive images of two-parent black families. The latter are harder to find. And since that was what my book was about, together we chose a different image— a mother and father holding the hands of their beloved daughter.

From slavery to the present day the black family in the United States has been primarily represented in a negative light by unenlightened mainstream culture that is utterly biased in the direction of white supremacist capitalist patriarchy. Indeed the survival of black family life in the context of slavery was possible precisely because the displaced Africans enslaved in the so-called New World had no concept of a nuclear family; they did, however, understand kinship—a circle of kin. And indeed that is the vision of family that allowed enslaved black folks to become surrogate mothers and fathers for one another. Again we rely on slave narratives for amazing stories of families striving to keep both their biological and chosen kin together in the midst of an oppressive society, which actively worked to keep slaves from building community with one another. Slave rebellion and resistance would never have been possible had black people been unable to build deep and abiding connections to one another.

We have only to examine what has happened around the world in the aftermath of cultural revolutions to have an idea of the chaos that must have occurred when slavery ended. Annals of history tell us that black people had diverse responses. Some folks immediately searched for and endeavored to reunite with family and kin; other folks reveled in the absolute freedom of no connections. Strategic detachment was one of the healthy psychological tools used by black folks so that they could endure the suffering of slavery with their humanity intact. But when slavery ended most folks wanted to create a stable world of family and community. However, the political system of white supremacist capitalist patriarchy made it difficult for free black people to set up nuclear families. Housing, food, and jobs were hard to come by. Black folks created what anthropologist Carol Stack would later describe as a communal culture of poverty where resources were shared and the survival of the collective was deemed more important than individual progress.

No one could study this history and not be amazed at the positive power of black families. Since many displaced Africans had come from cultures where families centered around matrilineal lines, the primacy of mother figures was sustained. Since slavery had created a structure where fathers were often not present (certainly the white slavers who were raping and impregnating black females were not sticking around to parent) and black males were often sold away from their biological family, it made absolute sense as a survival strategy for African Americans to arrange kinship circles around mother figures, as females were the only group doing parental caretaking.

Globally, the most common family system is a network of extended kin and community. This family system is a better structure to raise children in than an autocratic patriarchal family. However, in the early part of the twentieth century black people in the United States who had known the positive power of extended-family life were trying to emulate the standards set by white patriarchy. In that world it was the patriarchal nuclear unit that was normative and depicted as the only healthy family system. It is this point in African-American history where the black family begins to be characterized as problematic and unstable.

Since social science as an academic discipline was gaining prestige in the late 1900s, white sociologists began to bring their interpretations to bear on the black family: they labeled it unstable. Historians had already begun to debate the question of whether slavery had made it impossible for black family structures to emerge and be sustained. Sociologists, schooled as they were to be biased toward the patriarchal nuclear family, described extended kinship family systems as problematic even though they were working successfully. In keeping with the dictates of white supremacist domination, when white social scientists were asked to report on the quality of African-American life after the passing of the Civil Rights Act of 1964, they examined black families from a biased perspective. Reporting to the government, Daniel P. Moynihan stated:

> At the heart of the deterioration of the fabric of Negro society is the deterioration of the Negro family. It is this fundamental source of the weakness of the Negro community at the present time. . . . The white family has achieved a high degree of stability and it is maintaining that stability. By contrast, the family structure of lower-class Negroes is highly unstable, and in many urban centers is approaching complete breakdown.

Of course Moynihan and his colleagues were comparing lower-class black families to those of middle-class whites. Had he compared them to poor and indigent white families, it would have been most evident that poor black families were thriving better than lower-class whites despite difficulties. And had he compared middle-class white families to middle-class black families the positive resilience and strength of black families would have been apparent.

Of course because the report targeted lower-class black families, the system of white supremacy, patriarchy, and capitalism could still be idealized. Even though Moynihan used his report to call for more jobs for black males, he could have targeted capitalism for its impact on joblessness. By targeting the black family he made it seem as though the economic system was conducive to black progress and the failure lay with dominating black females in the home, whom he called matriarchs. Even though scholars at the time responded critically to his assessment, it became the public negative representation of the black family sanctioned by the government. In his book *Positively Black* Roger Abrahams boldly stated: "It is obvious to anyone who works with Negroes that they have a family system and that it has been remarkably stable, at least in terms of its configuration. It is unstable only when judged by the white ideals of the husband-wife-child relationship complex. Even more important is Moynihan's assumption that the stable family is the only social unit in which a child can effectively learn." But the scholars who called for an unbiased examination of black family life, one that would take into account the reality of class, did not rule, and the black family was systematically represented as unstable and problematic.

Depicting black family life as dysfunctional was a tremendous assault on the collective self-esteem of black people. It meant that from that moment on the quality of black American life would be determined not by the positive experiences of those black folks whose lives provided testimony that when given equal access to jobs, education, and housing black folks could thrive as well as anyone else but rather by the circumstances of those on the bottom. This failure to recognize the positive family life of black people created a false dichotomy that implied that the real black people were those on the bottom and the fake black people were those whose lives most closely resembled successful white peers. Black folks living in all-black class-stratified communities had always known that there was no monolithic black family. They also knew that there was a crucial difference between the life experiences of black folks with economic privilege and the life eperience of the have-nots. It was a blow to black folks to have positive black family life be deemed irrelevant and go unrecognized and an assault on the self-esteem and integrity of the black family.

Ironically, just at the historical moment when the black family was assailed by negative depictions, white women active in women's liberation were exposing the reality that white privileged-class families were indeed not internally stable. Corrupt male domination, domestic violence, incest, marital rape, and drug addiction were just a few of the problems feminist thinkers unveiled. In fact, these women were letting the world know that the privileged white family was not a stable unit, that if the children in those families thrived it was not necessarily due to the family unit. Of course they claimed that patriarchy rendered white families dysfunctional. Writing about the way patriarchy undermines the family in *Creating Love*, therapist John Bradshaw explains: "Patriarchy worked when life was tougher and basic security was everyone's concern." However, he points out that modern patriarchy promotes autocratic male rule in the family and leads to negative domination. Explaining further, he writes: "Patriarchal rules can be administered by women. Many women raised in patriarchal families are as controlling and repressive as their male models. Boys raised by such women can be seriously injured in their sense of masculinity. . . . But overall patriarchy violates women." Benevolent patriarchies are those where men rule, but without violent domination. This was the white middle-class *Leave It to Beaver* family ideal. However, the reality feminist white women exposed was a family tormented by male domination and psychological as well as physical terrorism.

This information, coupled with the growing awareness in the mental health industry that all was not "stable" in the white middle-class family, created a climate where new ways of thinking about family could emerge. As divorced rates soared, as economically privileged white women, straight and gay, chose to have children outside heterosexual marriage, ideas about the nature of families became less rigid, more progressive, and the notion that the nuclear family is the only family system that is positive was and is continually interrogated. Whether a mass-based audience is listening or not, feminist scholarship has thoroughly exposed the reality that patriarchy hurts families, that it stands in the way of love, that it is rarely a context where self-esteem flourishes. Speaking of his own past Bradshaw writes: "From their own patriarchal upbringing, my parents and relatives learned that love was based on power, control, secrecy, shame, repression of emotions, and conformity of one's will to the will of another, and of one's thoughts to the thoughts of another. These are not the bases for healthy human love." Even though feminist thinkers, myself among them, make the necessary connection between racism and sexism, it has had little impact on how the black family is depicted in our society.

Not nearly enough literature has been written examining the way in which the Moynihan report and the various ways it was used as an indictment of black family life created unprecedented gender conflict between black males and females. Both groups had struggled to develop healthy self-esteem in a culture where the required standards for gender roles established by institutionalized patriarchy were already way of out reach. If masculinity could only be achieved by protecting and providing for one's family, then under this system black men could never be "real" men. Concurrently, if femininity could only be achieved by the emotionally fragile, fair-skinned, long-haired angel in the house who is unable to work outside the home, then black women could never be "real" women. Prior to racial integration black folks developed their own modified versions of these standards, more fitting to the reality of black life. Had they not done so, no black families would have been places where healthy self-esteem could emerge.

Tragically, it was the moment black folks surrendered independent standards of black familial well-being and began to try to completely conform to the standards set by white supremacist capitalist patriarchy that the black family truly became and remains endangered. Since black males were the group who felt their identities threatened by the alternative gender arrangements black folks had been forced to create to ensure collective survival, they were the group most eager to embrace what is clearly now a fiction—the notion that if only black males could assume the role of patriarchal protector and provider the black family would become a stable, functioning unit. Or that if black males could be patriarchs in the fullest sense of the word their self-esteem would be assured.

A central characteristic of healthy self-esteem is the ability to be self-reliant and take responsibility. The moment white male patriarchs made it seem as though black male progress was being inhibited by dominating matriarchal black women, unenlightened black males were able to eschew responsibility for their own self-development, scapegoat black women, and assume the posture of helplessness, of victimhood. In response to the notion that black women had usurped black male power, many black males relied on male domination, particularly psychological and often physical abuse, to subjugate black women. Abandonment through excessive womanizing or simply leaving families were ways black men asserted their power over black women.

Ironically, the Moynihan report had made it seem that black women were antipatriarchal, hence his use of the word "matriarchy." In actuality, the vast majority of black females would have welcomed being able to conform to sexist-defined gender roles. Most black women did not have access to work that was liberatory and would have considered it a blessing to be able to remain at home. At no point in time in our nation's history has there been a huge body of black women who oppose patriarchy. Woman-hating men have been the group that has always tried to suggest that any self-supporting woman is antimale. But as Bradshaw pointed out in his analysis of patriarchy, women can be advocates of patriarchal thinking.

In the case of black women, whether married or single, most black females support patriarchal thinking, defined simply as social organization based on the belief that it is natural for men to have supremacy, to rule over others. It has been wrongly assumed that single black mothers repudiate patriarchal values. This is simply not the case. The self-esteem of many a young black boy has been wounded because he does not live up to the standards of patriarchal masculinity imposed upon him by his mother.

In many ways it is rather amazing to retrospectively see that black folk who had been so vigilant from slavery to the civil rights era about refusing to accept the racist white world's evaluation of their humanity suddenly by the end of the sixties were allowing white folks to define what was best for black family life. Black folks willingly accepted a version of black family life that made it seem that black females were the enemies of black males, a threat to their self-development and their self-esteem. Ultimately, sexism made it easier for both groups of men, white and black, to blame women rather than demand that white men assume responsibility for the myriad ways they exploited and oppressed black men, or for black men to assume responsibility for their failure to interrogate white supremacist capitalist patriarchy when it came to the role of the man in families, and for their failure to create alternatives.

Blaming black females and punishing them created psychological confusion in the minds of black women, whose ancestral legacy had been one of working alongside black men to achieve racial uplift. Now they were being told to be more subordinate. But what black females knew that the white social scientists who studied black life failed to see was that many black females already subordinated themselves to black men in the home even though they were the primary breadwinners. In my family, Dad was always the primary breadwinner. However, if social scientists had come to our house studying gender, they might have concluded that Mama was running the show, since it appeared that she made most of the decisions, did most of the talking. In actuality Dad was and is a pure patriarch and his word was law. He allowed Mama the appearance of being in charge much as a king sits on his throne and allows minions to do the work.

Most black females knew that the problem of black family life was not a refusal on the part of black women to be subordinate (lots of subordinate, do-anything-for-their-man black women were cruelly treated by black males). Yet fearing that there was truth in the notion that black females were keeping black men down, some black females worked even harder to assume traditional sexist feminine roles. I can truly testify that my mother waited on my dad hand and foot, did not work outside the home, was utterly feminine, supported him in every way, and he was still not satisfied. Despite these realities black females have not been able to completely squash the false and destructive notion that black women have stood in the way of black male progress. Quite the opposite is true: black women have been willing to go to grave lengths, even to sacrifice their lives, to make it possible for black males to get ahead.

Unfortunately, the devaluation of black womanhood has wreaked havoc on black female ability to cultivate healthy self-esteem. Since patriarchy denies females access to the ways of thinking that support psychological well-being, no black female, or any group of females in our nation, can achieve genuine healthy self-esteem without repudiating male domination. Nathaniel Branden was one of the first male self-help thinkers to realize this truth. In most of his work he writes about the need for women to be self-defining. In *Six Pillars of Self-Esteem* he contends: "Woman-as-inferior is not an idea that supports female self-esteem. Can anyone doubt that it has had a tragic effect on most women's view of themselves."

Branden recognizes early on the negative consequences for men who embrace patriarchal notions that their personal worth has to do with being a good provider. He concludes:

> If, traditionally, women "owe" men obedience,
> men "owe" women financial support and physical

protection. If a woman loses her job and can't find another, she has an economic problem to be sure, but she does not feel diminished as a woman. Men often feel emasculated. In hard times, women do not commit suicide because they cannot find work; men often do—because men have been trained to identify self-esteem with earning ability.

Cultural critic Barbara Ehrenreich called attention to the way in which the contemporary formation of the "playboy" masculine ideal was a repudiation of the notion that men prove their masculinity by providing and protecting. In its place white male patriarchs made sexual exploits the other arena in which a man could prove his masculinity. Unlike the notion of patriarchal masculinity as linking to earning power, which excludes masses of poor and indigent men, when masculinity was made synonymous with sexual predation men of all classes could engage in a level playing field. The playboy standard of masculinity gained greater cultural acceptance and currency in the sixties. And it had an enormous impact on black men.

Since the majority of black males could not count on getting a job, or once they acquired one, they were unlikely to work at a job paying wages substantial enough for them to support their families, they were more likely to look to sexual predation as the proving ground of their patriarchal masculinity. Hence the black male, who had, from slavery to the civil rights era, resisted being depicted in racist, sexist terms as a sexual predator, began in the sixties to wholeheartedly embrace this identity, deriving from it a pseudo self-esteem. Naturally, this had and continues to have disastrous consequences in black heterosexual relationships. Womanizing, and the deceit and betrayal that come in its wake, continually fuels the flames of the gender war between black males and females. Coupled with the misguided notion that black women stand in the way of black male progress, the sanctioning of sexual predation in diverse black communities has eroded the quality of family life. Black male sociologist Orlando Patterson in the extensive work *Rituals of Blood: Consequences of Slavery in Two American Centuries* documents the fact that across class black males engage in womanizing and sexual predation to the same degree. Since shaming and humiliation is usually a component of male domination in intimate matters, separation or divorce is usually the outcome of constant betrayal.

Patriarchal predatory masculinity has created a culture of intimate terrorism in the lives of black folks, which erodes commitment, trust, and constancy in all relationships, especially among heterosexuals. This circumstance has disastrous consequences for the development of self-esteem. Black females are often psychologically stuck in a state of self-doubt about their femininity and desirability. Black men who may on the surface appear to be proving their "patriarchal masculinity" by ongoing sexual predation actually experience the erosion of self-esteem that comes when an individual does not practice integrity. Through the assuming of an outer persona of "cool," black men have been able to fool themselves (i.e. engage in denial) and everyone else into believing that they are not suffering the loss of personal integrity. Indeed, much of the compulsive quality of black male sexual predation leads them to fill up all the spaces in their lives so there is no alone time when they might have to confront the emotional consequences of self-betraying behavior.

Increasingly, young black females are choosing to imitate the behavior of the male sexual predator. In an attempt not to be victimized by the sexist-defined gender roles that privilege males, they assume a patriarchal cool pose. Of course this means that a contemporary gender war is taking place that is far more alienating and brutal than any that have occurred in the past. The identification of all women as bitches and hos is a reinscription of old-style woman-hating patriarchy. What it leads to in black American life is more teenage pregnancy, rape, domestic violence, and the emotional shutdown of both females and males, both of whom suffer from crippling low self-esteem. Foolishly, many black leaders have responded to this gender warfare by falling back on fundamentalist religious teachings, urging young people not to have sex. This is foolish because it simply does not work.

Clearly, if adult men and women are in conflict and engaging in all manner of dysfunctional behavior, children suffer the fallout. More than 50 percent of black children are abandoned by fathers. Single and divorced mothers working overtime to provide economically while attempting to create a measure of emotional well-being in family life are simply stressed out and often depressed. Since the extended kinship structures, which at one time offered black children sanctuary and avenues where they could receive parental care whether their biological parents were present or not, have been eroded by liberal individualism, the emotional neglect of black children has almost become the accepted norm. This neglect often leads to child abuse when parents or parental caregivers are dysfunctional.

Today, black families (like all other families) are more in crisis than ever before in our nation's history because the levels of isolation and alienation are daily intensifying, as is the confusion around gender roles. In mainstream white culture gender roles have made radical shifts, and feminist challenges to patriarchy have produced a measure of equal opportunity, however relative. Every day white folks are revising notions of the family to encompass changes (for example, the number of gay people who are parenting, the huge numbers of people who are choosing adoption). Only conservative right-wing folks continue to act as though the patriarchal nuclear family is the only family system in which to raise healthy children. In light of the overwhelming evidence that the patriarchy is far more likely to be a damaging institution than a nurturing one, many folks have begun to look for concrete alternatives. All the evidence indicates that children raised in loving homes, be that two-parent families or single-parent homes, are far more likely to have healthy self-esteem and be fulfilled in their lives than children raised in chaotic, corrupt, dysfunctional environments.

Black families suffer more than those of other groups because black male leaders, often relying on fundamentalist religious teachings, continue to act as though the institution of patriarchy and its concomitant male domination will heal the crisis in black family life, willfully ignoring all the evidence that suggests patriarchy does not serve as a healthy or stable foundation for familial bonding. Overall black males and females have collectively refused to face the fact that the black family, in all its diversity, will never become a healthy functional context for bonding until patriarchy is critiqued, challenged, and changed. Sexist scholars continue to create work that falsely suggests that the presence of black males in the home would stabilize black families. These scholars often spend so much time studying and evaluating single parents (to prove how "bad" this family system is) that they never test out their theories by examining the self-esteem of children raised in dysfunctional two-parent families. Often success is measured by the degree to which individuals conform to the status quo (work, marriage, etc.). Yet self-esteem can be lacking in folks who are successful, who make lots of money, who maintain long-term marriages.

Until our nation wholeheartedly recognizes that healthy families are created in a loving environment, dysfunctional families will continue to be the norm. Patriarchal male domination in families stands in the way of love. When one adds to this deprivation, poverty, racism, the ravages of addiction, dysfunction will be the order of the day. If black families are to become places where self-esteem can flourish, gender warfare has to end. The constant scapegoating that takes place in a racialized sexist context, where black males and females "blame" one another for their failure to be self-actualized, must be replaced by the willingness to be responsible and accountable. Most important, until we can all recognize that love is the only foundation that will sustain a healthy family system, black families will continue to suffer from the toxic misinformation that distorts reality and makes it appear that all that is needed for black families to heal is a man in the house. Black folks need love in the house. And the presence of love will serve to stabilize and sustain bonds.

10

Easing the Pain: Addiction

Addiction erodes self-esteem. In recent years black Americans of all classes, and especially the lower classes, have experienced the devastation caused by widespread addiction. Now and then mainstream mass media focuses, on drug addiction in African-American life, but there has been no consolidated look at the way in which addiction in general has undermined the social stability of black American life. While social scientists are willing to expound about the impact of poverty and overwhelming joblessness in black communities, very few scholars pay attention to the impact of addiction to sugar, alcohol, tobacco, drugs, shopping, food, and sex or some combination of these mood-altering addictions.

Black leaders go on and on about the crisis in black America and never mention addiction. Critics who talk about the crisis in black families rarely talk about addiction and when they do they focus solely on drugs. In *Healing the Shame That Binds You* therapist John Bradshaw argues that we need to recognize a range of compulsive addiction to understand that there are a lot more addicts than most people realize. He contends, "We so often limit this area by over-focusing on alcohol and drug abuse. Pia Mellody has defined addiction as 'any process used to avoid or take away intolerable reality.' Because it takes away intolerable pain. It does so much for us that it takes time and energy from the other aspects of our life. It thus has life-damaging consequences." Bradshaw cites shame as central to addictive behavior.

Black people living in an imperialist, white supremacist, capitalist, patriarchal culture are daily subjected to shaming. The entire world of advertising and mass media in general, which sends both the covert and overt message that blackness is negative, is part of the propaganda machinery of shaming. No black child who watches television every day for even a few hours can escape the indoctrination of white supremacist–based aesthetics that relentlessly convey the message that to be black or dark-skinned is to be defective, flawed. Of course there are many positive interventions that can send a countermessage to a child, but those interventions are not happening in most homes. To the extent that black children are consistently shamed during the early years when they are developing a core identity, a core sense of self, whether that shaming comes from dysfunctional parental caregivers or the consistent pedagogy of a black-hating mass media, they are predisposed to become addicts.

Poor children of all races, and particularly poor black children, are often placed in front of television sets from birth on. They are encouraged by their addiction to television to crave all the products they see promoted there. And one has only to go to any poor black neighborhood when schools let out to witness the overwhelming consumption of sugar via candy and soda pop.

Many poor black children are overweight. Since shame about the black body has already been taught by the white supremacist aesthetics coming from white media, when fat is added to the picture in a culture where thinness is seen as both a sign of beauty and a sign of well-being, then children suffer. Psychiatrists Grier and Cobbs made this point in *Black Rage:* "Black children have been simply too vulnerable to the ordinary misery of learning about themselves and the world. The child who eats too much is in danger of developing a doubly enforced feeling of self-depreciation: fat (black), ugly (black), grotesque." In many homes, regardless of class, parents cope with the cravings produced by sugar addiction, but struggle is harder for parents who are overworked, underpaid, and emotionally distressed.

Among poor and working-class folks, buying a child sweets is much cheaper than meeting other material longings, all of which have been and are stimulated by advertising. Parents, especially teenage parents who may be addicted themselves, use sweets to pacify small children. Early on in life these children are learning that whenever they have an undesirable feeling, an uncomfortable feeling, they can alter their mood by eating excessive sugar. Bradshaw shares the insight that: "There are myriad ways to mood-alter. Any way of mood-altering pain is potentially addictive. It takes away your gnawing discomfort, it will be your highest priority and your most important relationship." There is no one who lives in a traditional black neighborhood who has not witnessed children who cannot concentrate more than sixty seconds on a book or in the classroom but who are utterly absorbed when licking their lollipops or eating a chocolate bar, so absorbed that they have blocked out the world.

Novelist Toni Morrison captures the seductive connection between addiction, sweets, and internalized racial self-hatred in *The Bluest Eye.* Pecola, the self-hating little black girl, is described by her mother Pauline Breedlove when still a baby as "a cross between a puppy and a dying man. But I knowed

she was ugly. Head full of pretty hair, but Lord she was ugly."
Writing about the contempt the white male grocer directs at
Pecola when she comes to buy the Mary Jane candy that she
loves, Morrison portrays the mood-altering nature of the
sweet. After Pecola buys the candy and moves outside, away
from the contemptuous gaze of the shopkeeper, she feels the
"inexplicable shame ebb," and when it returns she represses it
by focusing attention on the pleasure she will get from the
Mary Jane candy. Morrison writes:

> Each pale yellow wrapper has a picture on it. A
> picture of little Mary Jane, for whom the candy is
> named. Smiling white face. Blonde hair in gentle
> disarray, blue eyes looking at her out of a world of
> clean comfort. The eyes are petulant, mischievous.
> To Pecola they are simply pretty. She eats the candy,
> and its sweetness is good. To eat the candy is some-
> how to eat the eyes, eat Mary Jane. Love Mary Jane.
> Be Mary Jane. Three pennies had bought her nine
> lovely orgasms with Mary Jane.

This is a description of toxic shame at work. It links the negative self-esteem engendered by racism to compulsive addictive
behavior.

Much of the popular literature on self-esteem says very
little if anything at all about addiction. Perhaps authors assume
it would be obvious that addicts suffer from wounded self-
concepts because addiction is damaging and self-destructive.
It is the antithesis of all that is needed to have healthy self-
esteem.

All black people, whether poor or privileged, live in a world
that daily assaults their self-esteem. And when that self-esteem

has never taken root in the soul to begin with, each assault simply diminishes the possibility that healthy self-esteem will emerge. Entering their teens and young adulthood lives with ruptured self-esteem, many black folks continue a downward spiral into addiction. More than any other threat drug addiction, with the violence that it brings in its wake, has destroyed many poor black communities that were quite stable before they turned into war zones where drug lords fight to protect turf, where women and men prostitute themselves to satisfy addictions. When militant black power intervention failed to eliminate white supremacy, many black folks fell into deep nihilism and despair. Addiction soothed the chronic pain. It was and remains the mark of trauma, a symptom of the widespread emotional pain that was becoming all-pervasive in many black communities.

Bradshaw's insistence that "the drivenness in any addiction is about the ruptured self, the belief that one is flawed as a person" is particularly applicable to the lives of black folks. Despite incredible gains in civil rights in the public arena, in their private lives many black folks confront their own destabilizing shame.

In *Rituals of Blood* Orlando Patterson discusses the tremendous isolation many black folks experience, describing them as "the loneliest of all Americans." Bradshaw sees addiction as an attempt at overcoming loneliness, at knowing intimacy. He contends: "The workaholic with his work, or the alcoholic with his booze, are having a love affair. Each one mood-alters to avoid the feeling of loneliness and hurt in the underbelly of shame. Each addictive acting out creates life-damaging consequences which create more shame." Nothing could be more true for the drug addict in African-American life. Living in small segregated neighborhoods where their addiction is usually not hidden or is unmasked because the life-damaging behavior has become so grave, the African-American drug addict is usually scorned by self and community. Today's drug addict is a predator. Lacking adequate resources to satisfy a habit that is endlessly demanding, whether starting out poor, middle class, or wealthy, ultimately the addict must prey on the world around him to satisfy his cravings. For all these drug addicts, family and familiar community are the targets when all other avenues fail.

Ultimately, however, it is poor black people who lack access to the resources that might help them heal. Their broken self-esteem is intensified. And there is little they can do to heal. Bradshaw states:

> Shame begets shame. The cycle begins with the false belief system that all addicts have, that no one would want them or love them as they are. In fact, addicts can't love themselves. They are an object of scorn to themselves. This deep internalized shame gives rise to distorted thinking. The distorted thinking can be reduced to the belief that I'll be okay if I drink, eat, have sex, get more money, work harder, etc. . . . Worth is measured on the outside, never on the inside.

This shaming self is depicted by Richard Pryor in the film *JoJo Dancer,* based on his own intimate knowledge of addiction, by showing how the self splits off into voices that encourage the addiction by further shaming.

Usually the shaming voices reproduced in the mind of the addict are those of dysfunctional family members, who may have told the addicted person repeatedly when he was young that he was worthless, ugly, stupid, etc. These voices terrorize the addict, who has, in most cases, been driven to addiction in the first place by the longing to escape them. Chronic emotional pain leads the individual to seek solace. Addiction offers solace. The recent film *Monster's Ball* offers a painfully graphic portrayal of a black boy's addiction to sweets. Shamed and emotionally neglected, he eats sweets as a way to be self-solacing.

Contemporary therapists such as James Hillman and others have written about the way in which addiction manifests as a negative expression of spiritual longing. This analysis seems especially true for the multitude of African Americans who have left the church because it did not satisfy the needs of the spirit but who found and find no other avenues. In *Creating Love* Bradshaw contends that the toxically shamed individual has a mystified soul that is "marred by violence and the defensive trances it develops in order to survive." Suggesting that individuals who cannot satisfy the needs of the soul in healthy ways look to addiction both as a way to reenact abuse or be abused, he emphasizes the positive aspect of this longing. He contends: "The soul uses a kind of perverse spirituality to make itself heard in seeking ecstasy; addicts follow the urging of their soul, of their spiritual nature." Following this urge usually has life-damaging consequences. The substance becomes the god that the addict worships. Since addiction is not about relatedness, it cannot further connection or strengthen community; ultimately it estranges and alienates the user from the love that could be life-saving.

Black people addicted to food, alcohol, or drugs are often allowed to remain in denial because the communities they live in are hostile to the notion that one might use medical intervention to heal. Fundamentalist Christianity places so much emphasis on the power of the human will that many Christians are shamed when they attempt to acknowledge the need of outside intervention. It is this type of religious fascism that is detrimental to self-esteem, since it seeks to deprive the ruptured self of the resources that would enable wholeness and healing. The results of a national survey conducted by psychologist Valeria Watkins to examine why many black females who are clinically depressed do not seek help showed that most individuals were invested in the notion that they should be "strong," relying either on individual human will or divine will to rescue them. Tragically, they see seeking help as a sign of weakness.

Many black folks who are deeply depressed but unwilling or unable to seek mental care rely on food, tobacco, alcohol, and drugs to provide the space of solace. This is especially true for female addicts. And since women of all classes continue to be the primary caregivers for children, families suffer from the ravages of addiction. Testimony from women in Susan Boyd's book *Mothers and Illicit Drugs* reveals that individuals are often aware of the emotional pain that they seek to ease by using substances and are as aware of the difficulty in taking responsibility for their behavior because they fear hostile shaming feedback. Diane, one of the interview subjects, explains,

> The worst thing you can be in this society is a drug addict or a drug pusher. I think it is a harder thing to overcome than being a murderer. When you look at sentences, people who traffic drugs, who are addicts and who are trafficking to keep themselves going. They end up with more time than people who molest children. . . . I think they think that people who become addicted are weak

Inner Wounds:
Abuse and Abandonment

Chronic emotional pain prevents many African Americans from experiencing healthy self-esteem. To heal that pain it must be first identified, openly talked about, and claimed. Much of that pain is caused by the trauma of abandonment. It begins with the struggle to define self and identity in a world where loss is commonplace. In *Salvation: Black People and Love* I write: "Whether we take as the foundation of our psychohistory the African explorers who came to the so-called New World before Columbus, the free individuals who came in small numbers as immigrants, or the large population of black people who were enslaved and brought here against their will, this is an emotional backdrop full of the drama of union and reunion, of loss and abandonment." Too often black folks have felt the need to deny the reality of loss in their lives.

Often folks who are economically successful and have prestigious careers are the individuals who are most invested in maintaining a monolithic notion of the psychological impact of oppression and domination in our lives. They are only interested in narratives of triumph, which suggest that no matter the hardships and sufferings, black people have endured and overcome. Of course the reality is more complex. There are those of us who experience bouts of psychological distress but are able to heal and restore our souls. However, while some of us have managed to triumph, to endure and overcome, many more black folks are struggling to achieve even a small degree of psychological well-being. These are the individuals who experience chronic emotional pain.

From the onset of our lives in this nation black people have had to cope with unhealthy levels of anxiety. Enslaved black people underwent both the trauma of separation and were either victims of brutal oppressive violence or witnessed acts of violence. These abuses created a psychological post-traumatic stress disorder that to this day has not been adequately addressed. In recent times individual black nationalists have attempted to discuss this issue. For example Shahrazad Ali's book *Are You Still a Slave?* is basically shallow, but she makes useful comments about post-traumatic stress. Rightly, she contends:

> Acute and Post-traumatic Stress Syndrome occurs after severe physical and/or emotional trauma such as what our ancestors experienced during slavery. . . . We experience delayed onset manifested by our feelings of inadequacy, intense fear, self-hatred, feelings of helplessness, loss of control, and perceived threats of annihilation. Post-traumatic Stress Syndrome can be experienced by one individual after a traumatic event, or by large groups of people who shared a trauma by way of inheritability. This conclusion is based on more detailed study into the psychodynamics of post-traumatic stress which include self-defeating

behavior, guilt, depression, loss of personal relationships, no sense of personal identity, and disassociation and depersonalization.

Significantly, the trauma of white supremacist
assault on black folks began in slavery yet it has
been the extent to which the assault continues in
various forms that has made full collective psychological recovery difficult, particularly in the area of
self-esteem.

Racism and the fear of racist assault leads many black people
to live in a state of chronic anxiety and dread. Whether they
are responding to an actual state of siege or not, the feelings
are real. And in many cases the threat of assault is real. For
example, while black males no longer fear being lynched,
black males irrespective of their class experience anxiety if
they are being watched by white authority figures, especially
police. And while many nonblack viewers of the police brutality directed at Rodney King may have been and remain
unmoved by the injustice they witnessed, for many black viewers, especially black males, the witnessing of this traumatic
assault on tape was a reminder that this might happen to
them if they are not vigilant.

Hypervigilance is characteristic of trauma survivors. It is a
breeding ground for distrust, paranoia, and anxiety. Often the
loved ones of black men feel excessive anxiety if they know
their men are in an environment where they are likely to
encounter policemen or just any violent, angry white man.
None of us can or should forget the black undercover police-
man who was critically injured when shot by white colleagues
who simply assumed he was the criminal and not the white
person he was trying to apprehend.

In Judith Herman's important book *Trauma and Recovery: The Aftermath of Violence—From Domestic Abuse to Political Terror* she stresses that "the repitition of trauma amplifies all the hyperarousal symptoms of post-traumatic stress disorder." Living in a constant state of dread causes intense fear. Herman contends: "Chronically traumatized people are continually hypervigilant, anxious, and agitated." In this nation folks began to take post-traumatic stress disorder seriously only in the last twenty years. However, black people are often ridiculed and mocked when we attempt to apply theories of post-traumatic stress to our lives.

When black people discuss this issue, they often refer to slavery, which seems to many people, including black folks, like something that happened so long ago that it should not really impinge much on the present. It impinges on the present because many of the psychological difficulties black people faced during slavery and at its end were simply not addressed and because so much of the brutal trauma experienced then as a result of white supremacist assault continues to happen in different forms today. Whether it is the bombing of a church where black children are murdered, police stopping all black men in a northern city because a white woman claimed that a black male took her children, the freeing of a black male after years of imprisonment for a rape he did not commit, the dying Klansman confessing the torture of a black man he and others threw from a bridge to his death, or the state-sanctioned bombing of a home where black folks, including infants and small children, reside, dreadful crimes motivated by racism continue to happen and go unpunished; justice does not prevail. These incidents may only affect a small number of black folks, but they send a message to all of us that we are not safe, that no matter how free we are, white supremacy is alive and well.

The racially based anxiety of black folks receives little or no attention. When I wrote an essay a few years ago, "Representations of Whiteness in the Black Imagination," which examined black folks' fear of whiteness, white readers responded with shock that black people might fear white people. White supremacist propaganda in mass media sends the message that blackness is to be feared. In everyday life, more and more, white people act as though individual black folks constitute a threat to their safety and well-being even though most white people in our society have never been shamed, humiliated, slighted, attacked, or assaulted by a black person. Documenting the fear Americans have of the wrong things, in his book *The Culture of Fear,* Barry Glassner includes a chapter on black males that begins with the statement:

> Journalists, politicians, and other opinion leaders foster fears about particular groups of people both by what they play up and what they play down. Consider Americans' fears of black men. These are perpetuated by the excessive attention paid to dangers that a small percentage of African-American men create for other people and by a relative lack of attention to dangers that a majority of black men face themselves.

He highlights the fact that black men are more at risk for dying from a life-threatening disease, homicide, or suicide, that black men suffer ongoing economic discrimination (college-educated black males earn only as much as white male high-school graduates), and that black males are more often casualties of crimes than they are perpetrators.

Subjected daily to misrepresentation of the reality most

black folks experience by a white supremacist mass media, it is not surprising that black people may have a feeling of powerlessness over our destiny whether it is true to our experience or not. Inability to shape how we see ourselves and how others see us is one of the major blows to collective self-esteem. As individuals many of us feel we have more control, but we do live with the shadow of the cultural negatives that inform how we are seen by other groups. Clearly, when mass-based protest against racism was strong, black people felt psychologically stronger.

The murder of black leaders, the fact that civil rights struggle did not eliminate racism, that white supremacy in all its forms did not end, all led to a collective grief and despair in the African-American psyche that has not been resolved. When Malcolm X and Martin Luther King, Jr., were assassinated, that collective grief was felt throughout the nation. The fact that new visionary charismatic leaders have not risen to carry forth antiracist struggle depresses the spirit of that generation of black folks who wholeheartedly believed in democratic ideals, who believed equality was possible.

Racist backlash followed in the wake of all the marvelous gains of civil rights. And black folks began to feel despair about whether they could ever live in a world without racism. Books such as Ellis Cose's *The Rage of a Privileged Class* document the reality that opportunities abound for black people to flourish in myriad ways (academically, economically, etc.), but no amount of success brings racism to an end or prevents one from possibly being a target. When this racialized despair mingles with the grief about the death tolls in black life from violence, addiction, and life-threatening illness, that grief intensifies.

Concurrently many of the psychological traumas black

people experience as a consequence of racism merge with other traumatic experiences that have nothing to do with race, but together they intensify the psychic pain. Seeing race and racism as the only context for understanding the emotional crises that affect African Americans is problematic. Since attention is accorded the issue of race, psychological traumas inflicted by situations and circumstances that are not influenced or affected directly or indirectly by race get ignored.

Abandonment causes psychological trauma. Many black folks experience abandonment in childhood by parents who disappear, by parents who are present but abusive. Therapist John Bradshaw sees abuse as an essential feature of the dysfunctional family. In *Healing the Shame That Binds You* he states: "All forms of child abuse are forms of abandonment. . . . Abuse is abandonment because when children are abused, no one is there for them. . . . In each act of abuse the child is shamed." Across class more than 50 percent of black children are abandoned by their fathers. Ellis Cose suggests the numbers are even higher. In many homes where single moms are overworked and underpaid, depression abounds. The psychologically defeated parent is likely to be dysfunctional and abusive.

One of the insanities that prevails among many black Americans is the assumption that the active presence of fathers in parental caretaking is not vital and important, essential to a child's well-being. Sexist thinking continues to be the ideology that leads black folks to feel that the role of fathers in parenting is not as important as the role of mothers; this is just not true. Many black men are absent fathers because they have been socialized to believe their presence does not matter. Until all black people can acknowledge that the presence of caring fathers is essential in the formation of a child's healthy self-esteem and core identity, we will not be able to address issues of abandonment.

Oftentimes black females feel that the presence of fathers is unimportant because males, when present, act out, usually by being psychologically or physically abusive. The presence of violent fathers is way more harmful to a family than an absent father whose absence is understood and grieved. While many black mothers understand that it is better not to have a violent male in the home, they may not recognize that it is important to attend to the psychological wound that is inflicted by a father's absence.

Tragically, many absent black fathers were abandoned by their own fathers as boys. In far too many cases boys (and girls too) made contact with fathers who refused to recognize them, who shamed or humiliated them through aggressive teasing. In many black homes where fathers are present, whether occasionally or all the time, they may believe their primary role in the family is to be disciplinarians. They may use beatings and verbal harassment to try to make a child obey rules. These are forms of abuse that lead children to emotionally detach from fathers.

In many black families where physical abuse and sexual abuse would be responded to with outrage, emotional abuse is an accepted norm. Emotional abuse is the most common form of abuse that most of us experience. Therapist John Bradshaw identifies it as the most common form of child abuse. He highlights the fact that sexual and physical abuse are emotionally abusing but that in addition "emotional abuse includes the shaming of all emotions, name calling and labeling, judgments, and sadistic teasing." Black people often brag about sadistic teasing and valorize it under the heading of a cultural cool by calling it "signifying." When children respond to verbal abuse by acknowledging their pain, by whimpering or crying, they are often told to shut up or they will be given something to cry about. This demand that they repress true feeling and don a mask is a mark of soul murder and damages self-esteem. Negative signifying is assaultive and undermines fragile self-esteem. In many black families it is often females, especially mothers, who are the most verbally abusive and shaming. This shaming usually takes the form of sadistic teasing.

Mothers who are emotionally distressed, overworked and underpaid, are way more likely to emotionally neglect children. That neglect can evolve into abuse. Black children, like all children, often respond to abuse by emotional detachment, by simply shutting down. And as Bradshaw has stated, "we cannot heal what we cannot feel." If black children, girls and boys, learn to shut down emotionally early as a way of coping with the trauma of abandonment, then it will be harder to recover the lost self, the wounded inner child.

Writing about separations in early childhood in *Necessary Losses,* Judith Viorst explains:

> Most normal separations, within the context of a stable, caring relationship, aren't likely to leave scars on the brain. . . . But when separation imperils that early attachment, it is difficult to build confidence, to build trust, to acquire the conviction that throughout the course of our lives we will—and deserve to—find others to meet our needs. And when our first connections are unreliable or broken or impaired, we may transfer that experience, and our responses to that experience. . . . Fearful of separation, we establish . . . anxious and angry attachments.

These are the psychological states that may overdetermine the outcome of attempts to form intimacy among African Americans. Yet there is little or no discussion of the politics of loss in black life.

Before liberal individualism became the norm, before the individual two-parent or one-parent household became a norm in black life, folks often lived in extended families, in close-knit communities. In this cultural context a father or mother might be absent in a family but a child might emotionally connect with uncles and aunts, grandparents, or other relatives who would help them heal the wound of that absence by giving care, by acting as surrogate parents. The invention of public housing, which is a post-sixties phenomenon, destroyed much of this extended-family context in black life. It created a social context where young single parents could afford to abandon connections, especially with elders who might intervene in dysfunctional behavior. Within extended-family circles a child had a much greater chance of getting emotional needs met. In these environments single mothers were able to have support and care, thus having space for their own emotional renewal. Many black children, like other children in our society, are emotionally neglected because there is no one who attends to their emotional needs.

We may hear about the way black males are disenfranchised by lack of employment, but no one ever talks about the fact that unemployed black males could be trained to be excellent parental caregivers. State-supported wages for parental caregiving could bring more males, especially black males, into the home. This vision could only be fruitfully realized if sexist thinking were no longer the norm. Ideally, if black male parenting became identified with cool behavior, with a masculine ideal, more black men would seek to make parental connections. Despite all the wisdom feminist thinking and scholarship has offered about the value of male parenting, most black folks continue to believe that the primary role the black male can play in families is as economic provider. In reality black children would be far better situated to develop healthy self-esteem if they had loving fathers in their lives, whether those fathers work or not.

Many black males are unable to love because they are frozen in time, trapped in the abuses visited upon them as children. There is no literature that attempts to show how black males cope with traumatic abuse and abandonment. Recent books such as Ellis Cose's *The Envy of the World* that claim to explain black masculinity say little about the impact of early childhood trauma. In fact, black children are far more likely to be the victims of soul murder.

In *Creating Love* Bradshaw highlights the reality that the abused child often enters a trance state, one of hypervigilance, and in such a state a child may experience panic attacks, over-reactivity, or excessive worrying. He further states: "A child with unresolved trauma is frozen in time. When any experience resembling the old trauma occurs, the old trauma is activated. They experience the old threat in all its fearful potential." According to Bradshaw abuse survivors learn that "relationships are based on power, control, secrecy, shame, isolation and distance." These traits accurately describe the way many black folks, female and male, think about relationships.

Anger and rage are often the primary emotions that are expressed in intimate relations between black people, thus intensifying and normalizing black-on-black violence. In *Rituals of Blood* Orlando Patterson highlights surveys that show that not only do "Afro-American women get angry more often with a family member than other groups of persons but the anger lasts longer." And overall the survey showed that "Afro-Americans of both genders are getting angry with loved ones to a far greater degree than other people and women are sixty-two percent more likely to be the ones feeling the pain." Anger has rapidly become the only acceptable emotion for black people to express, so normative that it is often seen as synonymous with blackness by black and nonblack people alike. It disturbs me as I go about my life in one of the most diverse cities in the United States and am told by non-African Americans that folks think I am from another country because I am "nice, soft-spoken," so commonly does everyone associate black femaleness with rage and anger.

Rage addiction is the outcome of shame and anger. In *Healing the Shame That Binds You* Bradshaw identifies raging as one of the ways individuals create pseudo self-esteem. Anger feeds the empty void, giving the sense of presence. He explains: "When we are raging, we feel unified within—no longer split. We feel powerful. Everyone cowers in our presence. We no longer feel inadequate and defective. As long as we can get away with it, our rage becomes our mood alter of choice. We become rage addicts." This is certainly the case with many black males. And while black females may express anger more often in the family, it is black male rage that demolishes family.

In *The Envy of the World* Ellis Cose identifies black male rage as a primary factor that keeps black people from experiencing positive intimacy. He reports that "black men are more confrontational with their wives than white men; that violence (and it goes both ways) between black men and women is higher than for other races; that reported rates of infidelity are higher for black men than for whites; and that black men seem to be more demanding of—and less satisfied with—the women they have married." In describing negative rage in intimate relationships Cose makes the point that all the behaviors black men do with black female partners they also do with white and other nonblack partners. However, he does not identify the fact that sexism and woman-hating is often at the core of this mistreatment. To change this behavior black men would need to challenge sexism.

As long as black males and all black people view emotional detachment and the capacity to be numb, to shut down and withdraw, as positive characteristics of strength we cannot address and heal chronic pain. In *The Power of Soul* therapists Darlene Powell Hopson and Derek Hopson share the troubling insight that in many black families soulful expressions of joy and tenderness are often mocked and shamed. They contend, "People who are expressive, emotional, and demonstrative are viewed negatively. Control of emotions, being stoic and poised, is perceived as positive." Repression of emotions is precisely the state that can lead to explosions of anger and rage, particularly when those are the socially acceptable emotions. Negative emotions have gained currency in black life because they serve as the perfect mask for the false self. Black people, vulnerable and isolated, fear-based and in chronic pain, can wear the mask of confidence, appearing to be strong, together, intact, when in reality they are suffering.

Psychiatrists Grier and Cobbs chose to call their sixties' polemic on the issue of black mental health by the catchy title *Black Rage,* but much of what they wrote about was emotional pain caused by loss. In the conclusion to this book they declared:

> The grief and depression caused by the condition
> of black men in America is an unpopular reality to

the sufferers. They would rather see themselves in a more heroic posture and chide a disconsolate brother. They would like to point to their achievements (which in fact have been staggering); they would rather point to virtue (which has been shown in magnificent form by some blacks); they would point to bravery, fidelity, prudence, brilliance, creativity, all of which dark men have shown in abundance. But the overriding experience of the black American has been grief and sorrow and no man can deny that fact.

These psychiatrists offered no strategies that would help black folks cope with emotional distress. That was not the agenda of their polemic. It was more a manifesto proclaiming black defiance, proclaiming that black folks would take responsibility and attend to their emotional well-being.

Grier and Cobbs's vision of black folks addressing the myriad mental health issues that distress them in retrospect seems like mere utopian fantasy. In fact, as black folks gained a measure of equal access to money and consumerism, collective concern for antiracist struggle diminished and practically all discussions about mental health were silenced. Indeed much of the literature written about black folks in the post–civil rights era emphasized the need for jobs. Material advancement was deemed the pressing agenda. Mental health concerns were not a high priority. Even though issues of self-esteem were addressed as part of black power and black pride, the focus was shortlived given the nature of our psychohistory. We black folks continue to boast that we have triumphed over suffering rather than acknowledging that like any group of people who have been the historical victims of genocidal

the attention of whites to offer them in return sentimental syrupy affection. In fact, southern whites often required that black people behave this way in order to receive whatever favor they were willing to bestow.

Mama was not telling me that white people were not lovable; she was warning me that in the context of white supremacy giving one's heart to whiteness would be damaging and hurtful. For many black people in the post-desegregation years integrating and interacting peacefully with whites has required that they give their hearts to whiteness, and they have returned home brokenhearted. Integrated schools were the first place many black folks had the opportunity to develop a peer relationship with a white person wherein there existed a modicum of equality. Even though young black folks in predominantly white schools might receive the covert message that they could hang with the "in" white group but that their presence would always be provisional, they would choose not to get the message. It was a matter of survival. Assimilation and success in the white context often required denial.

One young black woman put it this way: "I really didn't see blackness in high school at all. I mean I was aware of how I was treated differently, but for so long my mom was always saying, 'You think you're white.' " She told her mother, "We don't see color here" and "They treat me the same." Over time, however, she became more aware that she was not treated the same and she confessed: "My self-esteem has gone down the toilet since I've been here. . . . Being made to feel that you're never quite good enough, never quite smart enough." This case, documented by Beverly Tatum's essay "Racial Identity Development and Relational Theory: The Case of Black Women in White Communities," is typical of the stories I hear from students on the predominantly white campuses where I teach.

Their stories are different from those of us who first racially integrated colleges where white folks mostly shunned interaction with us. We were there but often treated as though we were invisible. Or we shunned relationships with friendly whites for fear that they would be exploitative. There is now a generation of intelligent young black people who have entered white schools believing themselves to be the equal of their peers, believing even that racism does not exist. Their self-esteem plummets when they must face the reality that many of the white people who are kind and caring still harbor racist attitudes toward black people, often believing, with as much conviction as their overtly racist counterparts, that black people are inferior.

The work of white political scientist Andrew Hacker, especially his book *Two Nations: Black and White, Separate, Hostile, Unequal,* has documented the reality that a huge majority of white people in this nation believe that black folks are genetically inferior. Prior to integration many antiracist advocates believed that racial mingling would be the experiential proof that "people are people and race does not matter." But in fact many whites interacted with blacks, overcoming prejudices about socializing, without changing deeply held racist assumptions. While black children educated in predominantly white settings are more likely to have a diverse group of friends, they are also likely to have greater self-doubt about their worth and value.

Indeed, I began thinking about the question of self-esteem precisely because of the extreme levels of self-doubt I was witnessing in the black students I encountered at the Ivy League schools where I taught. Many of these students were coming from materially privileged homes where they were loved and cared for, yet education in an unenlightened predominantly white context had engendered in them a fear of not being worthy. Tatum identifies this as the "syndrome of not belonging," stating that "the pressures of trying to fit in, conform or communicate in the 'acceptable' form of the majority culture results in an anxiety that literally interferes with one's natural abilities and modes of expression." Often black folks enter these settings with fragile self-esteem already engendered by their internalization of white supremacist thinking. Tatum adds, "On many levels and at all ages the feeling or perception that 'you really don't belong' serves to complicate career aspirations in the forms of negative projection on one's self, overcompensation, assimilation, homogenization (trying to be like the one with perceived power), overaggressiveness, submissiveness, giving up, anger, isolation and even fears of failing or of succeeding." It is this feeling of not belonging that leads many black folks to self-segregate.

While self-segregating can create a more comfortable social setting, it does not heal ruptured self-esteem. All too frequently when black people choose to congregate with other black people, especially in a predominantly white setting, it is viewed as reverse discrimination, an expression of hostility. Sadly, in way too many cases it is a reflection of the longing to be away from the anxiety that is often present in a context with unenlightened whites, the fear of racial tension arising, the fear that one's fragile self-esteem may shatter. And it is a sign of positive self-care to remove oneself from any circumstance where there is danger of violation. I know of no cases where antiracist white people who have unlearned white supremacist thinking connect with black folks and are excluded.

Many of the tactics of psychological terrorism that patriarchal men use against women in intimate settings to maintain male domination are used by whites encountering a lone black person in an intimate setting. Often black people in such settings collude in their own shaming and humiliation because they have been socialized by internalized racism to feel "chosen," better than other black people. It is no accident that many of the recent books on race written by black conservatives give testimony in great detail about how nice white folks are to them and what hysterical liars other black people are to suggest that they are victimized by racial aggression in these friendly white settings.

In *Losing the Race* John McWhorter viciously castigates a number of black writers whom he sees as "guilty" of encouraging black people to see themselves as the victims of racist assaults that to his way of thinking are relatively rare. He provides an array of examples of "paranoid" black folks screaming racism where it just does not exist. Here is an example of his analysis:

> At Stanford University in the late 1980's, black undergraduates were surveyed as to whether they felt they were living on a racist campus. The survey was conducted in the wake of an incident in which two drunk white students living in the black theme house defaced a flyer for a talk on the possibility that Beethoven had black ancestry. They had made Beethoven's face on the flyer look black. Not the most gracious of pranks, but it was meant as a silly joke rather than a racist slur, and most of all, it was just one of those dopey little things.

While McWhorter is more than willing to be generous in his assessments of the motives of the white students, he seems unable to consider that he does not know what unresolved traumas involving race black students might have experienced that might have led them to feel threatened by this "dopey, silly joke."

Certainly, I have taught young Jewish students who express feelings of dread when looking at tattoos that are not swastikas but look like them. Their dread and fear is not because they think this is comparable to a Nazi holocaust but because of a psychohistory of remembered trauma that has been passed down, that has taught them to be ever on the alert. Their "hypervigilance," like that of the black students, may seem reactive but it has a reality base.

McWhorter, like so many self-proclaimed black conservatives who see themselves as exposing the stupidity of other black people, never seems to veer in his analysis very far from the negative stereotypes white people have already described, written, and proclaimed for generations. Here are his concluding comments about the Stanford incident: "If the systematic racism the black students sensed came from a perception that whites live in a separate world, this view was actively maintained less by the white community than the black, a great many of whom displayed a hostile wariness of white people. Most of the white students were baffled at the hostility of so many of the black students."

There is no large black student body on any predominantly white campus. In these environments individual black students, professors, and staff members are often isolated. Isolation makes us hyperaware and vulnerable. And indeed it may lead us to register a hurt more intensely than in a circumstance where we feel safe, as though we belong, as though everyone believes we have a right to be there.

There are many incidents where black people are victimized by racist assaults that are accepted as so commonplace as to not be worthy of note. No group of people in the United States has been as forgiving, or asked to be as forgiving, of assaults on the integrity of their being as African Americans. And even though there are times when an individual black person mistakenly claims victimhood, overall the vast majority of black people in the United States rarely assert any protest when their rights and their persons are violated by racist assumptions and racist acts. This lack of healthy self-assertion is itself an indicator of a diminished self-esteem. Often the problem is not that individual black people cry "racism" when no racism exists but that the cry comes from a place of pathological narcissism rather than of strategic organized meaningful protest. In McWhorter's book the incidents involving him that he sees as racism are not that different from the accounts given by the folks he mocks and ridicules; it's as though only the racism that happens to him is real and valid.

Nathaniel Branden makes the useful point in *Six Pillars of Self-Esteem* that asking questions and challenging authority are acts of self-assertion. However, he states:

> Sometimes people who are essentially dependent and fearful choose a form of assertiveness that is self-destructive. It consists of reflexively saying "No!" when their interests would be better served by saying "Yes." Their only form of self-assertiveness is protest—whether it makes sense or not. . . . While healthy self-assertiveness requires the ability to say no, it is ultimately tested not by what we are against but by what we are for. . . . Self-

assertiveness asks that we not only oppose what we deplore but that we live and express our values.

Many young black people who feel victimized by racism are more willing to articulate the cause of their pain than to consider taking any action that would eliminate that cause. This is the behavior that is self-defeating and self-sabotaging.

Teaching at a predominantly white campus where there are few black students, I was asked to respond to the concerns of a young black male who felt his white peers simply ignored him. He reported that no one responded when he made comments in class; it was as though he had not spoken. And he says: "When someone sneezes, someone responds, but not if it's me." Socially he feels like an outcast. He came to me for advice about whether he should leave. My first response was to ask him why he chose this type of campus and what he imagined would happen socially. I asked him to identify the primary reason he came to college, which he identified as the desire to get a good education. Not only was he liking all his classes, learning a lot, his grades were excellent. I wanted him to take responsibility for the choice he had made. I asked him to consider the possibility that he might go to a campus with more black students or with white students with whom he had more in common where his social needs might be met but that he could hate his classes. Rather than trying to find an either/or solution to his issue, we sought a both/and answer. Could he stay where he was doing well academically and find ways to satisfy his social needs?

Some conservative thinkers might have discounted his insistence that he was the target of racial harassment, usually through sadistic teasing. I found it useful to accept his accounts and to encourage him to put them in proper perspective. He was clearly in pain though he did not seem himself as "victim" nor was he responding with irrational rage.

While much has been made of black folks' saying that they find racism in their social encounters with whites, little is stated about the fact that many black people look forward to such encounters because they truly believe white people will treat them as equals. Whiteness is so idealized in our nation, in this white supremacist, capitalist, patriarchal culture that we live in, that some black people create a fantasy bond. It is an illusion of connectedness to whiteness that does not really exist. And even when an individual black person in an unenlightened all-white setting is violated, he may strengthen his fantasy bonding. John Bradshaw explains: "Bonding to abuse is one of the most perplexing aspects of shame inducement. Abuse is usually unpredictable, a sort of random shock. Abuse lowers one's self-value and induces shame. As one loses more and more self-respect, one's world of choices and alternatives is diminished." Fantasy bonds lead individual black people to stay engaged with white folks who shame and humiliate them, who communicate to them that they see black people as inferior.

I have witnessed this type of bonding most in interracial romantic relationships where a white partner demeans the black partner repeatedly using racialized declarations. White females who accept abusive behavior from black men that they would not accept from white male peers often do so because they do not believe black males are capable of functioning with moral decency. They may find the indecent acts erotically titillating. When I explained to a young black male student that his white girlfriend who treated him like he was a pet, unable to care for any of his needs, was assaulting his integrity as an adult, he acknowledged that he felt something wrong about their relationship but did not know what it was. He had been taught to believe possessing a white female and having her service his needs was a sign of masculine power. He was not feeling powerful. He was feeling diminished. But even so he had difficulty breaking the fantasy bond, breaking the belief that white women know how to treat black men well.

All too often unenlightened white folks attempt to reinscribe in subtle ways a plantation economy in their relationships with black folks, however friendly. They attempt to symbolically re-create a situation where the black person services their needs. They may need to feel more powerful. Helping a needy black person can satisfy this need. Or how about the white girl who, uncertain about whether she is beautiful, chooses a black female sidekick with low self-esteem who worships her white counterpart, assuming a role almost like that of a ladies' maid in the court? The black girl provides the background for her white friend to constantly reaffirm her special beauty. Sometimes I call this process re-mammification. Somehow the relationship between white and black friends becomes one where subordination to whiteness is expressed by this covert demand that the black person must not only assume a secondary posture in the friendship but serve the needs of the white person. Often black men are chosen by powerful white women as partners. He imagines he is showing the world that he is worthy because he has a white female companion when she may be treating him like he is her sexual servant. The pain many black people have suffered in their attempts to create mutual intimacy with white people is one explanation for the wariness that is sometimes expressed. They may fear contact because they recognize that their self-esteem is already fragile and they do not want to risk further diminishment.

Insecure black people who suffer from internalized racism need spaces where they can openly acknowledge their hatred of blackness and their love of whiteness if they are to cease relying on pseudo self-esteem. They need to be able to speak openly about their inability to love blackness, about the fantasies they hold about whiteness. Working through many of the unrealistic expectations about how interactions with whiteness will transform their lives will no doubt mediate the resentment that often comes when their fantasies are not realized.

White and other nonblack friends and loved ones who are committed to antiracist action are not threatened by the rigorous challenge that may come in intimate relationships with black folks. Nor do they come to black folks expecting them to do the work of teaching them about blackness or about how they should behave. They recognize that mutual regard is the essence of a healthy, constructive interaction. When white people unlearn racist thinking and action, they can and do interact with black folks in ways that enhance black self-esteem.

Seeking Salvation

Even though the conditions for healthy self-esteem may not have been present in our childhoods, even though the psychohistory of slavery and continued racist assault are barriers to self-love, black folks can build healthy self-esteem at any moment in their lives. We can embody the six pillars of self-esteem as defined by Nathaniel Branden: self-acceptance, self-assertiveness, self-responsibility, living consciously, and living purposefully. There are three primary pressures that keep many black folks from choosing to build healthy self-esteem: religious teachings that overemphasize self-sacrifice, group tribal mentality wherein conformity becomes the measure of loyalty, and hedonistic desires for material goods that are seen as indicators of success.

Coming from fundamentalist religious traditions, whether Christian or Islamic, many black folks (even among those who are not active worshipers in any faith or who claim not to believe in God) still live lives governed by a voice in their head, the voice of ancestral legacy or time spent in religious institutions during their formative years, which tells them that self-will is wrong, that they will be considered good if they obey authorities. In *Creating Love* John Bradshaw calls this blind obedience "obedience without content," which means that "it is virtuous to obey no matter the content." Most important, it is this type of obedience that destroys inner life and makes it impossible for the individual to act with personal integrity or what Bradshaw calls "true conscience." Even though negative stereotypes abound that suggest black folks are innately willful, reckless, and rebellious, most black folks have been schooled in the art of obedience.

Bradshaw reminds us that:

> True conscience can only be formed on the inside. It is built on a foundation of inner strengths and good habits. Blind obedience and punishment force us to live by rules that are external to ourselves. The rules become internalized and function like posthypnotic trance voices. To form a conscience, we must test the rules we learned in childhood in the waters of experience. We ourselves must ultimately choose or reject the rules we internalize in childhood. When we choose them, they become our own.

The prisons in our nation are full of black people coming from disciplining and punishing religious traditions who are resisting in a self-damaging way the demand that they obey autocratic authority.

Black folks who disobey are usually "acting out," reacting against the voices that are stifling their inner growth. But the acting-out behavior does not indicate a healthy break with the demand that they bow to the will of authority. It is merely an expression of how deeply trapped and bound they feel to a tradition that says one will be excommunicated from the world of divine grace if one disobeys. Conformity is more the accepted norm in African-American life than gestures of independent thought and action. This is why so many creative folks, geniuses, artists, and critical thinkers often feel they must leave "blackness" behind if they are to flourish. Ironically, they often take the rigid attitudes about obedience and judgment into the nonblack worlds they inhabit. Their rigidity is tempered and mediated by the openness of the world around them and not by their actually becoming more open.

Within diverse black communities when an individual refuses to toe the line and obey they are usually isolated and ostracized. Isolation is a favored weapon of psychological terrorists globally. It breaks people's spirits. Many of the black folks deemed "heroes" and cultural icons, such as Martin Luther King, Jr., and Malcolm X, engaged in repeated acts of self-betrayal to maintain allegiance to a discipline-and-punish morality. Malcolm X felt that he was losing his mind when his "true conscience" forced him to break through denial and face the hypocrisy embedded in the Nation of Islam and its leaders. Black folks, individuals who had previously shown solidarity with him and the causes he represented, were willing to assassinate him, as punishment for disobeying orders. The few black men who executed Malcolm X represented the many who felt he did not have a right to live if he was not willing to obey patriarchal rule. This is the horrific expression of fundamentalist religiosity and the rule it upholds: Submit or suffer punishment; obey or die.

This type of religious mystification is quite compatible with tribal mentality. Throughout our history in this nation black folks have been encouraged to function like a tribe. Discussing tribal mentality, Branden concludes:

> The essence of the tribal mentality is one that makes the tribe as such the supreme good and den-

igrates the importance of the individual. It tends to view individuals as interchangeable units and to ignore or minimize the significance of differences between one human being and another. At its extreme, it sees the individual as hardly existing except in the network of tribal relationships, the individual by him or herself is nothing.

When black people were in dire distress because of imperialist white supremacist, capitalist, patriarchal oppression (during slavery, and the period of state-sanctioned apartheid euphemistically known as Jim Crow), it made sense to develop an us-against-them tribal mentality as a survival strategy. However, when these extreme conditions ceased and it became more apparent that we black people could be the enemies of our well-being in much the same manner as whites, our survival strategies should have undergone a change. They should have become more progressive, more sophisticated, but they did not.

In the absence of productive change two trends emerged in the post–civil rights era: the identification of blackness solely with the corrupt ethos and mores of lower-class black folks and the uncritical embrace of sexist-defined gender roles. Nothing attests more to the reality that a great many black folks were not living consciously or purposefully than the fact that when white folks, female and male (along with a few enlightened black folks), were recognizing the need to transform gender relations, to challenge patriarchy, and to critique sexism, black leaders were insisting that the only force that could save besieged black families was patriarchy. Support of sexist thinking especially became a rallying, unifying agenda, furthering the tribal mentality and gaining its greatest momentum during the Million Man March. Sexist roles keep females and males from creating healthy self-esteem. Until black folks accept this, generations of black children will be socialized to think in ways that will diminish their spirit and their well-being.

Many black male scholars who can speak and write eloquently about the tragic gender wars in black life, the intimate terrorism, refuse to consider that challenging patriarchy, changing the way we see masculinity, and focusing on self-esteem could create the conditions for positive change. For example, in Ellis Cose's work on black masculinity, *The Envy of The World,* he makes the point, made often by black male leaders, that young black males lack positive role models, stating that "when it comes to role models in school, boys begin at a disadvantage, that they are surrounded, for the most part, by women, whom they have no interest in emulating." Since it is sexism that leads young black boys to feel that they cannot really learn from or emulate black women who are the abundant role models, then it is the sexism that needs to be changed. To expend energy focusing on black male absence is the collusion with the existing systems of domination that dooms black boys.

Orlando Patterson offers in *Rituals of Blood* a complex narrative of the crisis in black gender relations. He dispels the misguided assumption that poverty is the reason for bitter bonds between black males and females, offering solid evidence to show that negative trends are as present among affluent black couples as they are among the have-nots. Yet not once does he consider that the salvation of black males and females may lie in rethinking sexist notions of gender identity. In the conclusion to the section of the book headed "Broken Bloodlines: Gender Relations and the Crisis of

Marriages and Families Among African-Americans" he writes:

> Afro-American men and women of all classes
> have a terribly troubled relationship. Slavery and
> the system of racial oppression engendered it, and
> poverty, economic insecurity, and lingering racism
> sustain it. But blaming these injustices alone will
> get them nowhere. Not only because it is Afro-
> Americans themselves, especially men, who now
> inflict these wounds upon themselves—through
> the ways they betray those who love them and bear
> their progeny; through the ways they bring up or
> abandon their children; through the ways they
> relate, or fail to relate, to each other; through the
> values and attitudes they cherish and the ones they
> choose to spurn; through their comforting ethnic
> myths about their neighborhoods; through their
> self-indulgences, denials and deceits—but because
> only they as individual men and women can find
> the antidote to heal themselves.

The healing antidote is the creation of healthy self-esteem.

Patterson highlights the fact that many of the black males and females who are trapped in patterns of intimate terrorism are reenacting models of behavior learned from source figures. Yet he shows his own attachment to mystification by his unwillingness to consider that a challenge and critique of patriarchy and the sexism it condones is at the heart of the problem. Overall, most black males are unwilling to critique sexism, because their constant claim that they have been "emasculated," unable to be patriarchs, is the one narrative that gets white male attention. Black men of all classes are fantasy bonded with their image of the rich and powerful white man who can do anything he wants without having to consider the rights of others. This is the one desire black males have that white men understand. It acts as a bridge, a meeting place across a chasm of differences of culture and style.

If black men were to give up their allegiance to sexism, they would be surrendering the one tie that binds them to white men, the one space where they are allied. The longing to maintain this bond has shown itself to be greater than the longing for healing, for self-esteem. Ultimately, if what black men want, if what they see as the only desirable image of goodness and the good life is full access to imperialist white supremacist, capitalist patriarchy, then their rallying cry is really "give me the money" and the power. And forget about self-esteem.

Tragically, if given a choice between healthy self-esteem and huge sums of money most black folks would take the money. We know this because it is precisely what has happened and is happening on all levels, whether it is the black male addict who pimps his girlfriend and parasitically has a life of leisure because his mama works; or the black mother on crack who sells her schoolgirl child to a white Wall Street guy to get the money for drugs; or the rapper who makes mega-bucks with songs urging black-on-black violence while promoting misogyny and woman-hating; or the hypocritical wealthy black celebrities who preach self-help while remaining mired in self-hatred, even to the point of refusing to hire black employees because they view them as incompetent; or the many highly paid black spokepeople who usher in unjust racist public policy; or the heretofore unknown scholars who come to fame and money by attacking black folks and reinforcing white supremacist rule; or the already wealthy black actors who degrade images of black people; the shared fantasy is a life of wealth and hedonistic excess. There is no vision of living simply, and living well. This is the betrayal that is the heart of the matter—the betrayal of the collective yearning for self-esteem.

We as black folks cannot collectively have healthy self-esteem if we are not willing to change long-held survival strategies and distorted visions of the good life that simply have not worked and will not work because they are corrupt, because they do not promote self-acceptance, self-assertion, and self-responsibility, living consciously or purposefully. The values of consumer-driven status and power encourage people to stay unconscious, to conform, to follow the leader and stay with the pack.

When concerned black male thinkers such as Patterson and Cose address the crisis of black male and female relationships, they choose to play the macho card of downplaying mental health issues. For example, in *The Envy of the World*, Cose writes: "It would, of course, be simplistic—and wrong—to try to reduce all our problems, all the conflicts we have as black women and men, to uses of self-esteem or self-worth." He does not explain what he means here; however, embedded in this comment is a denial of the huge role self-esteem plays in determining the quality of our lives and our intimate relationships. Cose follows this statement with the comment that "there are some other huge problems, and perhaps none is larger than those that revolve around abandonment." Our issues with abandonment inevitably take us back to the issue of self-worth, because to heal from the abuse of abandonment, individuals must learn the healthy self-esteem needed for self-love.

Sexism and patriarchy, which act to prevent males and

females from learning self-love rather than unquestioning allegiance to oppressive systems, cause a huge measure of the conflict between black males and females. Within imperialist, white supremacist, capitalist patriarchy many black females and males act like "unwanted children," desiring the attention of the all-powerful white godlike parental caregivers. This competing for place, whether real or symbolic, is rooted in the racist, sexist construction of black males and black females as the enemies of one another's well-being and their internalization of this faulty logic. To deny our choice as to whether we can passively absorb ways of thinking that are destructive to our well-being or vigilantly challenge and oppose them is to support the notion that we are always and only victims, and that is simply not the case. Most black males and females have just not been critically vigilant when it comes to protecting the foundations that we have on which to build healthy self-esteem.

The one place where all black people can create an oppositional worldview, a theory and practice of well-being that does not need the support of any outside structure, is in our intimate lives, in our homes. Rather than making our intimate lives the locations of spiritual resistance where we defy imperialist white supremacist, capitalist patriarchy collectively, we have allowed our homes to become battlegrounds where there is no foundation for healthy self-esteem. And yet if we do not lay the groundwork there, early on when black children are constructing their core identities, it becomes harder, not impossible but way more difficult, for us to repair damage done and lay the groundwork for self-esteem. Positively, there is a growing body of self-help literature, work by Iyanla Vanzant, Ernest Johnson, and many others, that offers strategies for self-healing. The most difficult task we face is motivating each other to choose healing.

Even though many of us are suffering, our pain is familiar, and new ways of doing things feel frightening. Those of us who have experienced abuse, which is different from neglect, have more work to do to heal. And this work requires that we go against the rules of the tribe, that we look to alternatives. Black males and females are offered very few visions of healing that are antisexist. La Francis Rodgers-Rose and James Rodgers have long tried to offer analysis that would help heal wounds. In their book *Strategies for Resolving Conflict in Black Male and Female Relationships* they urge us to be willing to critically examine our childhoods and our relationships to source figures in our families of origin. They state:

> We are dealing with hurt. Hurt from childhood that we carry over and yet don't understand and we've never resolved it. We run from it; so we constantly hurt ourselves. . . . When dealing with black male-female relationships, we have to bring self-concept and self-image into perspective. If the self-image is distorted, the relationship will be distorted.

The core problem between black females and males is a spiritual problem. It is a struggle against self-hatred and self-loathing. In *The Return of the Prodigal Son: A Story of Homecoming* Jesuit priest Henri Nouwen reminds us that the self-esteem issues black folks face are universally faced in our nation. Confessing his own inner struggles and sharing the insights that were the outcome of those struggles, he writes:

> Here lies the core of my spiritual struggle: the struggle against self-rejection, self-contempt, and

self-loathing. It is a fierce battle because the world and its demons conspire to make me think about myself as worthless, useless, and negligible. Many consumerist economies stay afloat by manipulating the low self-esteem of their consumers and by creating spiritual expectation through material means. As long as I am kept "small," I can easily be seduced to buy things, meet people, or go places that promise a radical change in self-concept even though they are totally incapable of bringing this about.

Black women and men are urged by the dictates of white supremacist, capitalist patriarchy to remain small. Collectively we can resist this urge. We can challenge the systems of thought that teach us that low self-esteem is virtuous.

Many of us have been taught early on in our lives distorted versions of religious thought that suggest that we can only ward off pride and conceit by being self-sacrificing. True religious teachings urge us to love ourselves as we are loved by the divine—to recognize our original goodness. Cose reminds readers that if black males want lives of emotional well-being they must have courage. His words are equally applicable to black females. To build self-esteem that recognizes that "our worth can only be determined by what we make of who we are, which requires us, for starters, to reject with every fiber of our being the pitiable figure the world would make of us and to discover our own true and better selves, patiently waiting, perhaps unseen, in the outer reaches of our imagination." While it is true that we can build healthy self-esteem individually, we need support and affirmation.

One of the reasons it has been so difficult for black people to change our intimate bonds with one another is that we see very few progressive representations of black male-female relationships. Here I am not simply referring to romantic bonds. I am talking about all bonds of intimacy across gender. As a cultural critic I witnessed mainstream white culture make radical changes in gender roles but normalize those changes, yes, even make them sexy, by creating movies and television programs that affirmed men and women doing things differently. While unenlightened black folks are running around debating whether black single moms can raise a healthy child and attacking the small benefits these families receive from public aid, white folks are bragging about blended families, extended families, creating a public narrative of loving single mothers who choose to parent. This is the work black females and males must do to collectively create a foundation where they can mutually affirm healthy self-esteem.

Black males and females in relationships where they are daily reenacting abuse need strategies to heal that promote mutuality. We need a cultural campaign to undo the myth that we are each other's enemies. We need to remember the words of poet Wendell Berry: "We hurt and are hurt and have each other for healing." And we need to remember that love cannot take root in unequal relationships, in situations of domination. I do not know any black people who think we should love white folks who seek to dominate us; then we should not expect love to flourish between black males and females who seek to dominate and control one another. A radical recommitment to a love ethic is needed in diverse black communities, the return to living consciously and living purposefully that creates and sustains self-esteem.

14

A Revolution of Values

In the past few years I have found myself saying again and again that mental health is the revolutionary antiracist frontier African Americans must collectively explore. I have come to this conclusion because we are still facing problems that should have been solved long ago. While the onus for eradicating imperialist, white supremacist, capitalist patriarchy does not lie solely with black people, we are accountable to the world in which we live and move and have our being. And we, nobody else, have not done enough to make that world a place where all black folks can attain healthy self-esteem. In the construction of my own healthy self-esteem I have looked to the seers, critical thinkers, and writers who came before me to challenge me, to guide me, to light my path.

Organic intellectual, playwright, political activist Lorraine Hansberry is one of those chosen kin for me, one of those source figures whose life and work I have studied in the interest of inventing a world where I can grow and flourish and love myself. A white farm boy wrote her a letter in 1962 asking for her opinion on "the Negro Question." Replying with her characteristic wit and generosity of spirit, she explained to him that "the condition of our people dictates what can only be called revolutionary attitudes." Fueled by the antiracist militancy of the time, Hansberry declared that black people would need to create and define the nature of their struggles and their weaponry. Defiantly she declared:

> I think, then, that Negroes must concern themselves with every single means of struggle: legal, illegal, passive, active, violent and nonviolent. That they must harass, debate, petition, give money to court struggle, sit-in, lie-down, strike, boycott, sing hymns, pray on steps—and shoot from their windows when the racists come cruising through their communities.

When Lorraine Hansberry wrote these words I was ten years old. I read them for the first time when I left home to begin college.

Her boldness, her radical openness, excited me. A country girl raised in a strict fundamentalist dysfunctional home where no space was available for independent thinking, I was enchanted. She was telling me, not just telling, but teaching me, that collective black anger at injustice was essential, fueling the spirit of resistance needed for us to challenge and change white supremacy. I have read this passage often. But the words in this letter that stayed with me, that I know by heart, were boldly highlighted. With all the defiance of a manifesto they declared: "The acceptance of our present condition is the only form of extremism which discredits us before our children." These words stay with me because they remind me of the scope of our accountability as we struggle to end injustice. They remind me that black children have suffered and continue to suffer because grown people, of all races, but most especially black folks, have not created and sustained the cultural revolution that would make it simple, easy, the birthright of any black child, to be given the gift of a sound foundation for the building of healthy self-esteem.

When I read that the vast majority of black children are neglected, that more than 50 percent of black children are abandoned by their fathers, when I read about a large body of black children among the poor and homeless, when I read about the continued miseducation of black children that lets them graduate from high school without basic reading and writing skills, I am reminded of Hansberry's words. Who is to blame for this "soul murder"? Who is willing to be accountable? So much talk about race and racism and yet we have done so little to address the emotional suffering in the lives of black folks, a suffering that is felt most deeply, most intimately by black children. And already they have learned, even before they have learned words, how to formulate sentences; they have learned not to express what they feel, not to cry too loudly, not to reach for what they want, not to seek the affection they deserve.

Before they can even walk, many black children know what it feels like to be punished, to be coerced into obedience. They have been silenced by harsh, angry, shouting words their minds cannot even understand, but they hear the negative tones. They understand they are in danger. And they learn early to obey or be punished. They learn early to accept punishment as their fate, as the fate of someone born into the world unable to "act right." They learn early, intimately, deeply, the meaning of soul murder, that it is their destiny.

Do not think for even a minute that I am describing what happens to poor disenfranchised black children. Most black children of all classes learn early that they must obey or be punished. They learn early that if they are to survive they must learn the fine art of repression. Pioneer psychoanalyst Alice Miller devoted her working life to telling the world that the West has normalized child abuse. In *Banished Knowledge: Facing Childhood Injuries* Miller explains that learning repression to survive prepares a child to be dysfunctional, to fear a world where there is no room to question, and if there is no room to question, there is no room to learn. The independent thinking that is an aspect of self-esteem cannot flourish. Miller writes: "Much of what we have learned from earliest childhood, and continue hearing in later life, is sustained by this fear. Entwined with the fear is the idea that the child is basically something wicked which by means of our culture we should tame and turn into something better." This is the way most black children are viewed in our nation today, especially if they are the children of the poor, especially if their skin is dark.

Black folks raised in diverse black communities know how commonplace it is for black parents to brag about how well they use the system of discipline and punishment to make sure their children will be obedient. More than ten years ago in the book *Sisters of the Yam: Black Women and Self-Recovery* I addressed the way in which this type of parenting teaches repression, that it gives us black children who have learned only blind obedience and on the flip side blind rebellion—that is, permission to act out. The lengthy observations I made then are worth quoting:

> Fierce parental critique and the threat of punishment is a strategy many black women use to assert their authority with children. One has only to observe black women parenting young children in public places. Often the children are spoken to

harshly—"bring your ass over here like I told you, sit your black ass down and shut up"—not because the mother is angry at the children but because she desires them to behave "appropriately" in public settings. She wants to be perceived as a good parent. Notice though that being a good parent is made synonymous with the extent to which one is able to exercise control over a child's behavior. We would do well to connect this obsession with control to the strategies of domination white people have used, and still use, to maintain authority over us. The parent-child relationship in a culture of domination like this one is based on the assumption that the adult has the right to rule the child. It is a model of parenting that mirrors the master-slave relationship. Black parents' obsession with exercising control over children, making certain they are "obedient" is an expression of their distorted family relations. The parents' desire to "care" for the child is placed in competition with the perceived need to exercise control.

The misguided assumption that many people hold about single black mother–headed households is that the children have no discipline. The reality is more often than not just the opposite, that the children are rigidly disciplined, because obedience makes everything easier to organize—meals, sleeptime, getting off to school. Spontaneity and creativity threaten the order. Teenage parents are often the most vicious disciplinarians. Any setting where a parent is emotionally distressed, depressed, and at the same time overworked and underpaid is a breeding ground for dysfunction, which makes abuse possible. And when addiction, of any kind, to any substance (and that includes television), is added to the mix, emotional neglect will be the order of the day. The same is true for two-parent homes where dysfunction abounds. One of the most positive aspects of an emotionally healthy two-parent family is that if one parent feels emotionally unable to give appropriate care, the other parent is there to offer balance, to provide emotional nourishment.

Emotional needs have for a long time been regarded with disdain in diverse black communities. Leftover survival strategies learned in slavery and during other periods of intense racist oppression that taught black folks that it was important to wear a mask, to not show true feelings, are keeping a huge majority of black folks from attaining emotional well-being. Again and again in this book I have quoted therapist John Bradshaw's comment that "we cannot heal what we cannot feel." More often than not, across class, black folks view the expression of emotional feelings as weakness. Many of us have been taught that strength lies in the stoical representation of being unmoved, untouched, appearing "hard."

The demand that feelings be repressed begins in childhood. When I showed my hurt as a child, expressing emotional pain, I was sadistically teased. I was told repeatedly that I was "crazy" and would end up in a mental institution where no one would visit me. My parents wanted me to be less expressive of my emotions because they feared for my safety in the apartheid world we lived in. Like many black parents, they feared I might say or do the wrong thing in the presence of the wrong people (white authorities, or even a quick-to-take-offense black person) and suffer. They did not explain their reasons for insisting on repression when I was a child. Their admonishments did not take root, even with repeated physical punishment, because I simply did not accept their view of the world.

In *The Power of Self-Esteem* Nathaniel Branden offers the insight that some children survive painful childhoods with their self-esteem intact because they practice "strategic detachment." He explains:

> This is not the withdrawal from reality that leads to psychological disturbance, but rather an intuitively calibrated disengagement from noxious aspects of their family life or other aspects of their world. They somehow know, this is not all there is. They hold the belief that a better alternative exists somewhere and that someday they will find their way to it. They persevere in that idea. . . . This does not spare them suffering in the present, but it allows them not to be destroyed by it. Their strategic detachment does not guarantee that they will never know feelings of powerlessness, but it helps them not to be stuck there.

Reading way beyond my age level was the practice that gave me awareness that other ways of thinking about life existed, different from the ways of my parents and the world I knew most intimately.

I was one of seven children raised in a two-parent household where my patriarchal father was the primary breadwinner. In retrospect it is clear that Mama, whose role was to be the parental caregiver while Dad was to provide, had not been sufficiently cared for in her childhood, and she was afraid to make mistakes. She had to prove to the world that she could be the perfect homemaker. And above all else this meant to her maintaining order, a clean house, clean obedient children, clean on the outside and clean on the inside. Excessively controlling, invasive, domineering, Mama had no time to waste with emotional expression, with feelings. She took care of business. And she was not and is not happy. Like many black sacrificial mamas she realizes that her emotional needs have never been met. There are many mothers like her, the "strong" black women who have ensured our material survival and our material success.

In *Sister Friends*, a collection of personal testimony edited by Julia Chance and Michelle Agins, black women offer testimony to mothers like mine, who gave them important survival skills. The King sisters testify: "Our mother was a good mother. In other words, she kept the family together, but she was stern. She was very strict. We couldn't say anything. With our father, whatever he said went. There was no what he called 'talk back.' " The Shabazz sisters give testimony to growing up in a household full of dysfunction and their efforts to heal. Courageously, they share that their mother was a survivor of incest and rape. By the age of thirty-three she had seven children by different men, all of whom were absent. Abuse and abandonment shaped her world. The sisters see now that she was not emotionally available. Simbi recalls: "We were all just floundering in our feelings, not knowing what to do with them." Coming to recovery, these black women are claiming their healing. They have faced the pain of the past and find their healing in the present.

Significantly, it is important that we remember that many single black mothers are young. They are emotionally immature and/or emotionally disturbed. They cannot raise healthy children because they are not healthy. And poverty is not the issue. There are plenty of black folks raised in poverty in fam-

He's not a man, he is a little boy, and he needs to be allo he freedom to be a boy."

The notion that black boys are born "flawed and defective so pervasive in our society that grown black men have ecome the primary agents of repression, urging that black oys be taught through systems promoting a discipline and unishment model. Most of the folks who talk about special chools for black boys are advocates of a pedagogy of repres-on, where obedience to authority is the order of the day. I lways tell audiences that I never hear anyone but myself say, naybe black boys need Montessori schools where discipline is earned without threat of punishment.

Tragically, many black folks cannot imagine that one can earn discipline in other ways, that the threat of punishment s not needed. Black boys may do well in separate schools not ecause of harsh rules that demand they obey; they may thrive ecause they are receiving needed care and attention. I look orward to the day when we reclaim the love of black maleness hat is rooted in recognition of the essential goodness of black nales, a goodness that is present from birth. Many black boys vho are violent teens, and later on abusive and violent men, ave been taught from childhood on not to feel, to be emo-ionally numb. Cut off from the capacity to feel for them-elves, they cannot feel for others.

In *The Batterer: A Psychological Profile* Donald Dutton mphasizes that the emotionally repressed boy more often han not becomes an angry man, and patriarchy makes it pos-ible for him to transfer that anger to females, to scapegoat nd blame them. In black communities there is a tendency to lame mothers and to behave as though fathers have no role o play in creating emotional health for a child. Dutton mphasizes:

ilies where they were loved and cared for in ways that pro-moted the growth of their spirit and healthy self-esteem. If patriarchal leaders in this nation, male and female, continue to act as though poverty is innately unhealthy, the breeding ground for pathology, masses of folks are then psychologi-cally doomed, placed out of the circle of folks who can have access to emotional well-being. Poverty is an economic cir-cumstance that need not determine psychological well-being. All over the world people are dreadfully poor and yet have well-being.

The poor in our nation are daily assaulted by messages in mass media that say they are depraved, unworthy, criminal. In *Where We Stand: Class Matters* I argue that it has been a weapon of psychological terrorism for the materially privileged to equate poverty with worthlessness, to sell that image to the world and then ponder why the poor will lie, cheat, steal, and kill for symbols of status and success. Among poor children in our nation, especially the black poor, the message is taught early, "Your life has no value—you are doomed." The cynicism many black children learn is life-threatening. It destroys their capacity to hope.

Without hope they cannot rise to the challenge of strategic detachment, they cannot exercise their imaginations to do the necessary work of soul searching that would lead them to paths of healing. This loss of the ability to imagine is a char-acteristic of soul murder. It is present in the life of poor chil-dren but equally present in the lives of emotionally neglected and abused children in materially privileged households.

In a recent interview novelist Toni Morrison tells of sharing a book with a young girl, between the ages of ten and eleven, with a passion for gymnastics. When she talked to her about the true story of a girl whose parents put her on a clothesline to start her training early, the girl Morrison was talking with could not imagine it. Morrison recalls, "And I said, 'Just imagine it.' She said, 'No, I can't.' " Morrison reflects on the child's capacity to comprehend but her inability to use her imagination, stating:

> I was so depressed! She is a top-of-the-line student, but she cannot visualize. So then I started to do a little exploration, and I found that there are many young children who are watching *Teletubbies,* and having a good time, and learning to read fast, and building a good vocabulary, and making good grades—but they can't participate in the imaginative process.

Sadly, black children are often encouraged by parents to stop imagining, to "face reality."

When I first went on tour for my children's book *Happy to Be Nappy,* which is a playful story about black girls loving themselves, especially their natural hair, I was stunned when black parents shared with me their fear that this thinking could be dangerous. They felt that by teaching black children that the world hates their natural hair, they were preparing them for reality. This faulty logic has often been handed down in styles of black parenting where children have been traumatically forced to face negative reality in the name of preparing them to cope. This violates the child's spirit. Rather than learning, they may feel overwhelmed and shut down, disassociate, or just become tranced out and numb—all states of psychological shutdown. I told my audience that any black child who has a foundation of healthy self-esteem will not only possess the skills to face reality but will know how to cope

with negative and positive experiences. I urged the embrace the reality that when we teach black children class to have healthy self-esteem we prepare them to liv and well. We do not simply teach them how to survive to succeed. Many successful people are emotionally da children masquerading as adults, and in some areas o lives they are harming themselves or someone else.

Offering black children needed skills for health esteem means not only that we teach them to expre honor their feelings, but that we do not impose sexist roles that make it appear that boys should be sing and shamed if they have feelings. Often black boys emotionally expressive of their joy or their pain a ished, or taught that they cannot become men learning the art of repression. Underlying this in that they not be allowed a childhood is a hatred maleness that finds its expression in homophobia, t say, the feeling black boy child is often taught it is feel because that makes you gay. And gay is somethi hated. Imagine the soul murder taking place in a b who is destined to be homosexual. He is taught to feelings and to hate his sexuality.

The violence done to black boys is the abusive i imposed on them by family and by society, that they In my own family, a niece has a wonderfully intelle ative, gifted black boy who is in touch with his Already he has learned to question authority, to tal about any circumstance for which he has strong fee parents, especially his patriarchal dad, believe that h homosexual if he does not learn to control his emo does not learn "how to be a man." Mama, attemptir a wise intervention as an enlightened witness, kee

There is a pool of rage in such an individual that can find no expression—that is, until an intimate relationship occurs and with the emotional vulnerability that menaces his equilibrium, the mask he has so carefully crafted over the years. Perhaps it is the mask of a "tough guy," or a "cool guy," or a "gentleman." Whatever identity he had created is irrelevant. Now a woman threatens to go backstage and see him and his shame without the makeup. Then, to his own surprise, the rage starts.

Little black boys are daily being socialized to become grown men who batter by a patriarchal world that teaches them that they can only be real men if they give up the right to feel. Challenging patriarchy is essential to any quest to save black men. Sexism and patriarchy threaten the life of black boys and men because they teach them to deny who they are in the interest of maintaining male domination.

Increasingly, black girls are pressured to assume a patriarchal stance as well, to shut off their feelings to prove they can be as tough as any guy. Like their male counterparts these girls are being taught to accept violence as their nature and as the nature of the world around them. They cannot raise healthy children; they can only create monsters. Alice Miller reminds us that "the so called bad child becomes a bad adult and eventually creates a bad world." To refuse to accept the present condition this nation has placed black children in, we must be willing to face the truth, we must be willing to feel the pain.

Many black people, like other groups in this nation, believe that there is no essential goodness, that humans are born bad. While it is true that we are all born with the capacity to do good or to do evil, if the will to do good, to affirm life, was not a stronger will than the urge to destroy, humankind would have long ago wiped itself out. I share Alice Miller's vision when she writes: "It is not true that evil, destructiveness, and perversion inevitably form part of human existence, no matter how often this is maintained. But it is true that we are daily producing more evil, and with it, an ocean of suffering...that is absolutely avoidable. When one day the ignorance arising from childhood repression is eliminated and humanity has awakened, an end can be put to this production of evil."

Black children are often taught from birth on that they are "evil." The word "evil" is often used when parental shaming of the child occurs. But the more commonly used synonym is the word "bad." Often when a black child is showing curiosity about the world they are told not to touch, not to explore, that they are "bad" when they do.

When a teenage niece had a child, she understood that her girl was exceptionally bright and she was proud of this fact. But having a gifted child may require a parent to give more attention, and that parent can respond with irritability and annoyance. In the case of my niece for a short time she was just telling her daughter that she was "bad." When I asked my niece to describe the behavior she considered bad, it was all expressive of curiosity, of the will to know her world, to enlarge the scope of her imagination. Talking with her about the language she used, I asked her to consider saying, "You are a genius just like your aunt," and observe the impact or to simply affirm the rightness of curiosity and exploration by positively setting boundaries. When any child hears repeatedly that they are bad, even before they really know the meaning, a parent is encouraging, by the use of the term, damaged self-esteem.

Black children will continue to suffer assaults on their self-concept if there are no enlightened witnesses who intervene and lay the groundwork for self-esteem to flourish. Our nation is not and has never been a child-loving culture. Increasingly it is a culture that devalues the life of black children, that represents that life as disposable. Even the advocates for black children are often blinded by their own allegiance to negative styles of parenting that highlight discipline and punishment. If we want black boys and girls to survive with integrity, with dignity, with the capacity to know joy, then we recognize that more than anything else they need to be loved. That love can thrive even when there are scarce material resources. Love is the key to changing and transforming the self-concepts of black children; it creates the path to self-esteem.

15

Recovery: A Labor of Love

Everyone in our nation must confront difficulties when faced with the task of creating healthy self-esteem. I began this book talking about the fact that one of the pioneer voices writing on the subject of self-esteem, psychotherapist Nathaniel Branden, started his investigations in the late fifties, working with patients who were more often than not white, well-educated, and from materially privileged backgrounds. Remembering this period of his life, Branden recalls the difficulties he faced as he endeavored to engage his colleagues about the issue. He recalls:

> No one debated the subject's importance. No one denied that if ways could be found to raise the level of a person's self-esteem, any number of positive consequences would follow. "But how do you raise an adult's self-esteem?" was a question I heard more than once, with a note of skepticism that it could be done. As was evident from their writings, the issue—and the challenge—were largely ignored.

Significantly, Branden's work showed and shows that the struggle to develop healthy self-esteem is universal in our nation.

During the late sixties when Branden was highlighting the importance of self-esteem, black folks had just begun to talk about the ways in which white supremacy and racism make it all the more difficult for black people to develop healthy self-esteem. White supremacist thinking rooted in Western metaphysical dualism socialized citizens of this nation to think in binaries—superior/inferior, good/bad, black/white. This was the ideological rationale for domination permeating our nation's religious thought and shaping its most powerful institutions. Racism was the organizational principle around which white supremacy was institutionalized and maintained. Sixties, black leaders, both civil rights advocates and the more militant antiracist black power activists, agreed that it was difficult but not impossible for black folks to create healthy self-esteem even if nothing changed about the system of domination exploiting and oppressing us. By calling attention to the issue of self-esteem they hoped to create a cultural climate where black folks would pay particular attention to their psychological well-being.

In the introduction to *Six Pillars of Self-Esteem* Branden declares: "Apart from disturbances whose roots are biological, I cannot think of a single psychological problem—from anxiety and depression, to underachievement in school or at work, to fear of intimacy, happiness, or success, to alcohol or drug abuse, to spouse battering or child molestation, to codependency and sexual disorders, to passivity and chronic aimlessness, to suicide and crimes of violence—that is not traceable, at least in part, to the problem of deficient self-esteem. Of all the judgments we pass in life, none is as important as the one we pass on ourselves." All of these issues are faced by black people. And yet our need for self-esteem has been mainly talked about in relationship to race and racism.

As a consequence, as black folks gained greater civil rights, as racial integration became the norm in the workplace and less problematic in housing, conservative and radical black leaders abandoned their short-lived focus on self-esteem.

As more and more black people were encouraged to assume that the only culprit preventing growth and development in black life was racism and that primary solutions to the problems we faced were jobs and money, the issue of psychological well-being was either abandoned or talked about solely in terms of racism. In the same year that Nathanel Branden published his first book on self-esteem, psychiatrists William Grier and Price Cobbs published their bestseller *Black Rage*. They began their chapter on "Mental Illness and Treatment" insisting that there was no evidence to suggest "that black people function differently psychologically from anyone else" and "psychological principles understood first in the study of the white race are true no matter what the man's color." To them racism was the factor requiring a different approach to the mental health ills of black folks; for the therapists to help they needed both to understand racism and to be capable of offering strategies for healing that would correspond with the lived reality of black folks.

Grier and Cobbs had been trained in a conservative approach to psychotherapy that deemed the task of the therapist to create a "change in the inner world" that would correspond with the capacity to make a positive "adaptation to the world outside." One of the primary themes of their book was that black folks would be damaged if they made peace with white supremacy and racism, and that their goal was to change the social order and not adapt to it. Courageously, these two black psychiatrists worked to make the kind of intervention in the existing social therapeutic order that would lead to the formation of a space where mentally ill black folks could be treated with respect and care.

A few years later in *The Jesus Bag* they were explaining why black patients distrusted therapy and, when seeking care, had begun to look for black therapists even as they voiced their skepticism about the role of therapy:

> Research in psychotherapy is in a sorry state and it is difficult to say precisely how many people are helped by black, white, yellow, or red therapists. . . . The black therapist considers himself primarily a healer and is content with such a definition, knowing that black people need healers. As a good therapist, he never ignores the most pressing issue of the moment. If a patient's house is aflame, he puts it out. If his patient has a physical ailment, he sees that it is cared for. If his patient is hungry, he sees that he is fed; if he is cold, he sees that he is warmed; and if his patient is threatened, he extends a shield-arm of protection, knowing these are the sets which define one human's benevolent involvement with another, and convinced that only within such a matrix of love and concern can any psychological treatment flourish.

These heroic mandates often masked the reality that black therapists often despaired of their capacity to help patients heal precisely because they could not change so many of the circumstances that had created the context for mental illness in the first place.

I emphasize the work of Grier and Cobbs because they were and to a grave extent remain the first therapists to reach a huge audience of black folks, male and female. And to some extent their pessimism about mental health care, about the reality of challenging and changing racism, may have informed the move away from any consideration of therapy as a useful place of healing for African Americans. Most African Americans had and have deep suspicions about the efficacy of therapy. They may see a black person who goes to therapy as weak, or they may decide that this person is not really black, since "black people do not go to therapy." Institutionalized health services were never transformed to consider the specific needs of patients whose mental health ailments were adversely affected by systems of domination, race, sex, or class. Poor people, of any race, in our nation rarely have access to the best therapeutic care. It is no wonder then that most black people remain cynical about mental health professionals.

Therapy is a useful and necessary place for healing. It is the one place in our society where emotional pain can be acknowledged without negative judgment and the desire for emotional well-being affirmed. But it can never be and should not be seen as the only site of healing. Since the most helpful therapy is often the most costly and the most difficult to find, it is essential for African Americans seeking mental health care to find the many paths to healing. Some of us seek strategies for healing in self-help literature, others in AA, or we go to the therapy that our insurance will pay for. Most black folks I talked with who went to therapists they did not choose, who were simply on their insurance plan, did not find these experiences helpful. Much healing happens in therapeutic conversations individuals have with caring loved ones (friends and family) or spiritual counselors.

Overall, though, there is a mental health crisis in African-American life. This crisis is most deeply felt around the issue of self-esteem. Until we can acknowledge this reality we cannot begin to adequately address it. Like the ·skeptical responses Nathaniel Branden heard initially from his colleagues, I find that many of my colleagues are willing to affirm that self-esteem is an issue but then express grave doubts about whether there are any solutions to the problem. I hear in their voices both skepticism and a hint of despair. Many of us black folks despair of our capacity to make meaningful life transformations that will create and sustain emotional well-being because we have been collectively "stuck" for so long. The stuckness is a reflex of learned helplessness, the fear that we cannot adequately address what ails us because we do not have the money or the power; this is the message we constantly hear from mass media.

The good news is that changes individual African Americans need to make do not require money or forms of power that are external to our being. These changes can be made by using the resources everyone already has available to them. We begin to create the foundation of healthy self-esteem by recognizing that we have the capacity to heal ourselves. One of the stumbling blocks to healing in black American life has been the assumption that we need someone, some force outside ourselves, to heal us. This can never and will never happen. Healing must come from within. This was the wisdom Toni Cade Bambara offered years ago when she was urging militant black male activists to critique sexism. Bambara reminds us: "Revolution begins with the self, in the self. The individual, the basic revolutionary unit, must be purged of poison and lies that assault the ego and threaten the heart." Bambara was directing us to do the work of building healthy self-esteem at the very beginning of the seventies. Her vision was clear and right on. And the people did not take it up and allow themselves to be guided by her wisdom and her light. The people wanted to project and talk about the enemy out there, the one they can scapegoat, rather than identify and confront the enemy within, the one we can control, challenge, and change.

As black folks we have been in a quandary for some time when it comes to our well-being. On one hand we are compelled by circumstance to identify the ways in which white supremacy and racism inform the development of our self-concepts even as we have to remain ever aware that our self-concepts are shaped by many other factors as well. Racism could be eliminated tomorrow and many black folks would still have to confront the issue of how to build healthy self-esteem. While the politics of race and racism clearly shape our relationship to loss, the fact is many folks are abused and abandoned even though they may have suffered very little direct racist assault. To a grave extent many black people have focused so much attention on racism that they have forgotten to look at life holistically; they have failed to see that race is a factor shaping our destiny along with a whole slew of other issues, and that if we want to get ourselves together we have to critically examine all the factors, not just race. We are encouraged to focus solely on race. Every day mass media sends the message to black people that the only aspect of their lives that is at all relevant and worth highlighting is race. And when black people internalize this they are left without the resources to know who they really are. Race matters. And at the same time race is not the only thing that matters.

Black people know this. We are encouraged to focus solely on race and live in denial of the truth about our lives. We are not encouraged to look at family-of-origin issues that may not have anything to do with race. We are not encouraged to look at patterns of sexuality and sexual abuse that may have nothing to do with race. We are still, despite the contributions of black women thinkers such as Toni Cade Bambara and Audre Lorde, debating whether we have a right to take a critical look at gender relations among African Americans, to challenge sexism. And when we tell people that revolutionary visionary feminist thinking might actually help us heal some of the gender-based mental illness in our diverse black communities, most folks just stop listening.

Bambara laid it out in her essay, "On the Issue of Role," and it is still painfully relevant. Speaking about rigid gender roles, she writes:

> Now, we tend to argue that all that is a lot of honky horseshit. But unfortunately, we have not been immune to the conditioning; we are just as jammed in the rigid confines of those basically oppressive socially contrived roles. For if a woman is tough, she's a rough mama, a strident bitch, a ballbreaker, a castrator. And if a man is at all sensitive, tender, spiritual, he's a faggot. And there is a dangerous trend observable in some of the movement to program sapphire out of her "evil" ways into a cover-up, shut-up, lay-back-and-be-cool obedience role. She is being assigned an unreal role of mute servant that supposedly neutralizes the acidic tension that exists between Black men and Black women. She is being encouraged—in the name of the revolution no less—to cultivate virtues that if listed would sound like the personality traits of a slave. . . . We have much, alas, to work against. The job of purging is staggering. It perhaps takes less

direction of healing. Exercise, positive thinking, and extending yourself on behalf of someone else's well-being are the three easiest ways to end depression, or if it's major league, taking these steps will bring you closer to finding the therapeutic care you need.

Positive thinking helped free enslaved black folks. And all the other struggles for civil rights that let us participate in the many freedoms we have today were fueled by positive thinking. Since we talk back so well, we need to talk back to negativity. Affirmations are great for building self-esteem. Give your children affirmations to say in the morning and at night. Traditionally, black people made affirmations a central feature of prayer. I began my day with the affirmation, "I am breaking with old patterns and moving forward with my life."

Prayer and meditation help us heal. We prepare ourselves for both by learning to be still and be quiet. And with meditation we learn to breathe, to follow the life force in and out. And the other way we can move toward self-esteem is to surround ourselves with people who constructively contribute to our growth. Forgiveness of ourselves and others paves the way for self-acceptance, for learning to accept ourselves and others as we are, to drop the judgments.

The fact that racism continues to impact negatively on our lives as African Americans has led many of us to feel that we can never be free of suffering. That is a slave mentality, because it denies both our history and our own agency. We have to drop our addiction to suffering, to our complaint, whether it's about what white folks have done, or what your mama and daddy did, or what your man has done, or these children done done. We have to let the suffering go. And that's particularly difficult for those of us who have created life dramas out of suffering.

In *The Power of Now* Eckhart Tolle shares the insight that the best way to drop suffering is to focus on the Now, not to be dwelling on the past or the future. That means letting go of our addiction to dread, worry, and other negative states. Tolle writes: "Once you have identified with some form of negativity, you do not want to let go, and on a deeply unconscious level, you do not want positive change. It would threaten your identity as a depressed, angry, or hard-done-by person. You will then ignore, deny, or sabotage the positive in your life." We all know someone who is mired in negativity. Gently ask them to stop sharing the negative with themselves and with you.

Think about the six pillars of self-esteem and apply them to your life. Start with the issue of personal integrity. Branden says it means having principles of behavior and being true to them. It means keeping one's word, honoring one's commitments, being faithful to one's promises. Living consciously means cultivating awareness, asking the questions that make you a critical thinker: who, what, when, where, and why (children do this exceptionally well). Self-acceptance requires that we like ourselves just the way we are, and in that liking decide stuff we want to change. Self-responsibility means we are willing to "come correct" and be accountable for our actions, for what we say and what we do. Self-assertiveness lets us practice honoring our needs, wants, values, and judgments and find the right times and places to give them expression. And lastly, to live purposefully we look for the places of meaning in our lives. For some of us it's family bonds; for others it's working for a cause or just simply practicing kindness and compassion in everyday life.

Find the black people in your life who have healthy self-esteem and talk to them about what they did and do to be fulfilled and self-actualized. Imagine how differently our lives would be as black folks if from the time we were first born we were taught to cultivate self-esteem as the foundation for success, as the first step on the path toward fulfillment, toward living a joyous life.

Last, and most important, if we begin to practice love, defined here as a combination of care, commitment, knowledge, responsibility, respect, and trust, we have all the tools we need to build healthy self-esteem. Try it out when you are unsure about any decision you need to make in any area of your life by asking yourself just what love would tell you to do. Be guided by love and you will find the way to self-esteem.

16

Restoring Our Souls

Throughout this nation black people are experiencing a spiritual crisis. We are joined in this crisis by all who love justice, who yearn for peace, and long to live freely. This crisis is for many folks a crisis of values. Longtime believers in freedom and justice, many black folks have betrayed these beliefs in the interest of getting ahead, material gain, and the trappings of success. Greed, made manifest through the ongoing tyranny of addiction, has been the seductive force luring many black folks down the path of corruption, self-betrayal, and hard-heartedness. Whereas we were once a group that prided ourselves on recognizing the value of inner life, a life that could have meaning and joy even in the midst of struggle, oppression, and exploitation, many of us tossed those belief systems aside, believing that the real way to freedom was by giving in to the dictates of a culture of domination and surrendering one's moral and ethical stance.

This shift in collective African-American values was dramatized in Lorraine Hansberry's play *A Raisin in the Sun*. When Walter Lee wants to take the insurance money the family has received from the father's death and open a liquor store, Lena Younger bears witness to his greed and the desperate compulsive-addictive nature of his craving, and she asks him, "Since when did money become life?" He replies, "It was always life, Mama, but we just did not know it." Through this critical exchange Walter Lee remained true to the values of his upbringing, but he was a harbinger of things to come, ushering in a new way of thinking that would soon become the norm for many African Americans.

Gaining access to material plenty changed the worldview of African Americans from a communalist ethic that placed a high value on compassion, sharing, justice, to an ethic of individualism whose credo was "I've got mine, you have to get yours." Many African Americans saw this as the only response they could have when antiracist struggle did not win the day, when our leaders were assassinated, militant attempts to use force were crushed, and the democratic ideals we had believed in so wholeheartedly were exposed as shame for most of the nation's citizens, especially public officials. Collectively, African-American spirits were broken. And this mood of despair and heartache was felt most intimately among the poor and the underclass.

The response to this crisis of spirit was most often a turning away from life-sustaining values toward the forces of death that seemed all-powerful. Observing this ontological shift in the late seventies, Lerone Bennett published an article in *Ebony* magazine titled "The Crisis of the Black Spirit," warning:

> The danger is real and pressing. For the first time in our history, the inner fortresses of the Black Spirit are giving way. For the first time in history, we are threatened on the level of the spirit, on the level of our most precious possession, on the level of the soul. And what this means is that we are threatened today in this country as we have never been threat-

ened before. A Great Black Depression . . . is eroding the moral and spiritual foundations of Black culture. To come right out with it, we are losing a whole generation of people.

Bennett saw confronting and coping with this depression to be the "gravest challenge we have faced in this country since the end of slavery." Patriarchal leaders attempted to address this spiritual crisis by material means. The crisis has continued.

The spiritual emptiness that was rapidly creating genocidal havoc in black life has intensified. It mirrors the crisis in spirit that grips our nation. In *Ethics for the New Millennium* His Holiness the Dalai Lama offers the insight that all the people of the West have wrongly believed joy could be found solely through acquisition of goods. He contends:

> According to my understanding, our overemphasis on material gain reflects an underlying assumption that what it can buy, by itself alone, can provide us with the satisfaction we require. Yet by nature, the satisfaction material gain can provide us with will be limited to the level of the senses. . . . It is obvious that our needs transcend the sensual. The prevalence of anxiety, stress, confusion, uncertainty, and depression among those whose basic needs have been met is a clear indication of this. Our problems, both those we experience externally—such as wars, crime, and violence—and those we experience internally—our emotional and psychological sufferings—cannot be solved until we address this underlying neglect. That is why the

great movements of the last hundred years and more—democracy, liberalism, socialism—have all failed to deliver the universal benefits they were supposed to provide, despite many wonderful ideas. A revolution is called for, certainly. But not a political, an economic, or even a technical revolution. . . . What I propose is a spiritual revolution.

Like our nation as a whole, black folks are in need of a spiritual revolution that will enable us to collectively reclaim a way of being in the world that allows us to honor ourselves, to value ourselves rightly. Choosing spiritual revolution, black folks would reclaim the power of soul.

During the most intense periods of antiracist struggle in the United States, black Americans were charting a journey to freedom that exploited and oppressed peoples all over the world sought to follow. They wanted to be guided by the redemptive spirit, the celebration of life, that was ever present in the midst of African-American hardship, through suffering, and there in our moments of triumph. In the words of the gospel song often heard during those years of struggle, "Walk together children, talk together, don't you get weary, there is a great camp meeting in the promised land." The wounded people of the world admired African Americans not because we were so courageous or valiant; other folks fighting oppression had these traits. We were admired because through all our suffering we had held on to a joy in living that we identified as the outward manifestation of inner soulfulness.

In *The Jesus Bag* William Grier and Price Cobbs linked this soulfulness to a spirit of mystical transcendence, declaring: "Soul is the toughness born of hard times and the compassion oppressed people develop after centuries of sharing a loaf that is never enough. . . . Soul is the graceful survival under impossible circumstance." Researching black expressive culture in the late sixties, Roger Abrahams proclaimed:

> Soul is sass because sass is one of those actions which emphasize be-ing. It is also any act which confronts, which seizes initiative for the pleasure of finding energy and letting it throw you around. It is looseness, but it is also instant reaction. . . . It has an eternity of its own which resides in the moment of creation. Soul is willingness and resilience, but it is also pride in knowledge of the existence of this resilience, and so it is also an unwillingness to bend in those directions which don't feel right because to do so is to deny the existence of such a cultural style and integrity.

The philosophy of soulfulness advocated by so many black folks prior to desegregation was rooted in the experience of an oppressed people who survived and flourished because they cultivated the skills of compassion, cooperativeness, endurance, faith, and hope, coupled with the belief that joy could be given expression, and beauty could be found anywhere, even in the most negative circumstances. In other words, enslaved black folks wisely held and shared the belief that the soul must be cared for no matter the circumstance, because soul matters.

This philosophy of soul was and remains a life-sustaining principle. In *The Power of Soul* therapists Darlene and Derek Hopson state: "When we have an open, honest connection with soul, we are able and ready to live a full, satisfying life and to share it with others. Soul is our passion and power to express and act upon our innermost feelings and follow our divine mission." The philosophy of soulfulness as an ontological principle of being in African-American life offered a foundation of healthy self-esteem. By emphasizing the power of soul African Americans wisely reminded themselves and the world of the limitations of thinking through the power of body, of placing too much emphasis on race. Evoking the power of soul was a constant reminder that race was a manmade construction and that the limited outer covering of the body could not begin to define the scope of the soul's reach.

Embedded in the metaphysics of soul was the understanding that one had to strive for psychological wholeness. This vision of wholeness included the recognition that breaking the bonds of racial tyranny was necessary even as it reminded us that we would need to cultivate a sense of our selves, of our humanity, that went far beyond racial freedom to be whole. A metaphysics of soul offered, and offers, us a foundation for healthy self-esteem because we are reminded of our essential oneness with life. In Christian mysticism this is articulated via the recognition that God is love, that love is where we begin and end, that our essential humanity cannot be destroyed no matter what is done to us.

In *The Road to Peace* Henri Nouwen explains that "Ministry in a mystical sense involves an inner freedom that radiates and heals." Emphasizing, as enslaved black folks once did, that our true self is reflected in divine spirit, Nouwen writes, "We can love others because God first loves us. The spiritual life is coming into touch with that first love. . . . We can be a liberating and creative presence in the world only if we don't belong to the world, if we don't depend on the world for our real identity." Articulated here is the spiritual crisis that so many

African Americans confront. On the one hand they know that the world they are living in is white supremacist and racist; on the other, they look to that world to provide an identity, a reason for being. And it is no wonder then that they find only emptiness, that they feel lost.

Any African American who watches television for more than a few hours a week is daily ingesting toxic representations and poisonous pedagogy. Yet the ingestion of constant propaganda that teaches black people self-hate has become so much the norm that it is rarely questioned. When I ask my students, both African Americans and our nonblack allies in struggle, why they claim to be antiracist yet spend their money on movies that depict black folks embodying negative stereotypes straight out of slavery days, they want to argue that it is "just entertainment." It is a measure of collective low self-esteem that not only black folks have been brainwashed to be entertained by images that degrade but that the capacity to take delight in images that reveal the essential goodness of black people has been numbed. The arguments made about those images is that they do not represent real "blackness." This is our contemporary tragedy. It is marked by the trauma of losing one's soul.

Many contemporary black folks, especially young black people, are among the first to surrender the capacity to care for their souls by surrendering their ability to feel. Derek and Darlene Hopkins make this point in *The Power of Soul:*

> In some African-American families, soul is devalued, avoided, or even ridiculed. Personal expression is frowned upon. Parents may advise or order their children to distance themselves from black people who appear soulful, perhaps to the point where a

youngster feels embarrassed or humiliated by contact with soul and their inherent urge to express their experiences and inner feelings. People who are expressive, emotional, and demonstrative are viewed negatively. Control of emotions, being stoic and poised, is perceived as positive.

In many ways the insistence on soul murder is an expression of internalized self-hatred, since white power is perceived as inexpressive, cold, ruthless. To be without soul then is to be symbolically "white."

This seems especially ironic since so much of the assault on the soulfulness of African-American people has come from a white patriarchal, capitalist-dominated music industry, which essentially uses, with their consent and collusion, black bodies and voices to be the messengers of doom and death. Gangsta rap lets us know black life is worth nothing, that love does not exist among us, that no education for critical consciousness can save us if we are marked for death, that women's bodies are objects, to be used and discarded. The tragedy is not that this music exists, that it makes lots of money, but that there is no countercultural message that is equally powerful, that can capture the hearts and imaginations of young black folks who want to live, and live soulfully. It is no accident that black youth culture began to mix soulful lyrics with contemporary arrangements, because their souls yearn for a creativity that is life-giving and death-defying even as they must continue to push the mask of "cool pose."

The commodification of blackness and what was once thought of as distinct black culture was one of the ways the deeper spiritual aspects of soul became obscured. Soul as a metaphysics that enhanced the self-esteem of black people by power of soul, we find ways to self-actualize to be fulfilled. The power of soul fosters in us an awareness that we must care for the needs of our spirits and seek an emancipatory spirituality. The soul's guiding light still shines no matter the extent of our collective blindness. At any moment, at any time, we can turn toward this light to renew our spirits and restore our souls.

empowering them to struggle for justice, to practice love, was threatening to the forces of domination, to white supremacist, capitalist patriarchy. As Michael Lerner writes in *Spirit Matters:* "The capacity for self-transformation and inner healing is part of what we mean by having a soul—the soul is the part of us that energizes us to go for our highest ethical and spiritual vision of who we can be." When soulfulness gets turned into just another commodity to be bought and sold in the marketplace, its power to transform lives is diminished.

In white supremacist, capitalist, patriarchal culture, the power of soul was one of the few cultural and spiritual resources black folks possessed that many white folks envied. And it took no great conspiracy for that envy to seek to flatten out the meaning of soulfulness by acting as though it could be packaged and sold like any other material good. Black capitalists have been just as eager and as willing as their white counterparts to destroy the soulfulness that sustains life and replace it with a shallow sense of soul that makes material gain the only major signifier of progress. Better to turn black leaders like Martin Luther King, Jr., and Malcolm X into flat, sentimental icons, street signs, T-shirts, and holidays than to create an educational system that might offer young black people the reading and writing skills needed to study their works in their entirety. Of course accountability for soul murder does not lie solely with the young because the corruption they fall into has been sanctioned by unenlightened elders.

Martin Luther King, Jr., more so than any other black leader, repeatedly warned black folks, and all the citizens of this nation, that we risked soul murder by choosing imperialist power and material gain over love. In his sermon "The Man Who Was a Fool" he reminds us:

Our scientific power has outrun our spiritual power. We have guided missiles and misguided man. Like the rich man of old, we have foolishly minimized the internal of our lives and maximized the external. . . . We will not find peace in our generation until we learn anew that "a man's life consisteth not in the abundance of the things which he possesseth," but in those inner treasures of the spirit. . . . Our hope for creative living lies in our ability to establish the spiritual ends of our lives in personal character and social justice.

Embodying the power of soul in his work for justice, Martin Luther King, Jr., showed us what soul looks like when it is personally manifest in our being.

King's detractors have taken evil delight in exposing to the world that he was flawed, a man of contradictions. This was not news. King had consistently confessed his human frailty even if he did not explicitly name the content of what he deemed his sins. More important, the metaphysics of soul as understood by enslaved black folks and handed down through generations included an understanding that we cannot judge one another rightly, because we have neither the vision nor the holistic understanding to make meaningful judgments. The infinite compassion and will to forgive that was an essential characteristic of soul must be regained if we are to create soulful communities of resistance. Henri Nouwen reminds us that "Life without judgment is very difficult. It means trusting that new life can emerge even in a world full of distrust, violence, destruction, and war." This is another unique gift the power of soul offers—the opportunity to renew our faith in one another and restore our hope. Soul

enables us to dare to trust even though our trust has be betrayed again and again.

Knowing that care of the soul is essential for surviv the inherited wisdom that can provide us the metaph foundation on which to create healthy self-esteem the soul's agency that no regime can take away. In duction to *Care of the Soul: A Guide for Cultivating Sacredness in Everyday Life*, Thomas Moore " 'Soul' is not a thing, but a quality or a dimens encing life and ourselves. It has to do with relatedness, heart, and personal substance." care of the soul is not a method of problem tends:

In a way it is much more of a ch chotherapy because it has to do richly expressive and meaningf in society. It is also a challeng imagination from each of us problems at the feet of a posedly trained to solve t soul, we ourselves have sure of organizing an good of the soul.

Soulfulness is democra to the needs of our so

This vision of free principle in the liv metaphysical recc no matter the ci provided us w